MW00927920

31 Days to Coming Alive

Jennifer Hand

ii

WHAT OTHERS ARE SAYING:

Holley Gerth, Best-selling author of *You're Already Amazing, You Were Made for a God-sized Dream, You're Going to be Ok.* www.holleygerth.com

> Jennifer Hand is a woman who does more than talk about joy--she lives it. Her words will help you discover what life to the full really means and how you can experience a reawakening of your heart. Jesus has so much he wants to give you and this book will help you discover more of *all* you've truly been longing for deep inside.

Jan Silvious, Aauthor of *Fool Proofing your Life, Same Life New Story.* Speaker and life coach. www.jansilvious.com

> Jenn Hand is real. She speaks with the candor of one who ' knows.'
> She knows who she is.
> She knows who God is.
> She knows she loves Him well and
> She knows He loves her with an undying love.
>
> In *Coming Alive in 31 Days,* you will have an adventure in knowing God and knowing yourself that will breathe new life into your soul.
>
> Take the challenge to 'come alive' and I promise you in 31 days you will find new life surging through your being in ways you might never have expected!

iv

TABLE OF CONTENTS

ACKNOWLEDGEMENTS

It feels crazy that I am even writing this page. So the first person I want to acknowledge is my awesome dream giver— God. God who called me to write this book and follow this crazy God sized dream called Coming Alive.

Next.. my family. Mom and Dad: There are no words to describe how incredibly amazing you are. When God chose me to have you guys as parents, He chose the best. Thank you for teaching me to live alive. For all the family fun nights, yummy home cooked meals, quality time, hugs and love. For all the memories, laughter, things you taught me about Jesus, and especially how loved I always felt/feel. You are amazing. Michelle—I could not imagine not having had you as a "wombmate". Not many people get to be born with a best friend, but I was blessed with that. You teach me more about loving Jesus every day. Thanks for being such a cheerleader and my best friend. Todd, I am so blessed by you as my brother in law--- we can just say brother. You are one of the kindest servant hearted people I know.

To my Coming Alive board of directors family: Don and Debbie Sapp, Treesa Reeves, Diane Hundley, Hunter Dees, Shawna Hart, Michelle and Todd Humbert and Robin Casey. You guys were just crazy enough to say yes to helping me in this dream of Coming Alive Ministries. I never could have done this without you. I love our board "meetings" and I love how God shows up big. Thank your tireless work, your heart, and for providing the invitation to come alive. This is possible because you said YES!

To my Thursday night Bible study family, I love you my sisters more than I can find words to say. Thank you for showing up every Thursday to let me have a place to teach

2

the exciting things God is speaking. Thank you for your prayers, for laughing together and praying together. After all, when Thursday night ladies pray—God moves in a mighty way. I love you and I love how you make Thursdays the highlight of my week.

TJ Ellis: Thanks for letting me feature your beautiful writings in this book. Thanks for being a gift for me for all these years. Thanks for what you have taught me about faith.

To Mark Carpenter: I am so blessed that I was paired with you during my Richmont initial years. You have been a model spiritual director to me and have walked me deeper in my walk with the Lord then I can express. You modeled to me a wise counselor/spiritual director and have been a great mentor and friend. Thank you for the concepts that you taught me that come out in this book.

And to all of you who want to live alive in Christ, who share the message, the passion and the vision : THANKS. Thanks to those who donated to make this happen, to those who have faithfully supported, and for all of you have brought life into my life. I am beyond blessed.

FOREWORD

Everyone should have a friend like Jennifer Hand.

You know those people who make you laugh so hard you feel like you might pee yourself a little? Jenn is one of those kind of friends.

You know those people who ask *really* good questions (then actually want to know the answers)? Yup. Jenn is that too.

You know those people who always see things just a little differently…and in doing so stir curiosity, wonder, and excitement in you that you didn't even know you had? That's my friend, Jenn.

I've never known someone who exudes grace and humor so authentically and intentionally. These are tools in an artist's hands that elicit passion, inspire change, and tap into our deepest longings…always inviting us to *MORE*.

This is Jenn's gift to the world and the church.

Let's face it – we all need someone who can help us *come alive*! Whether it's stress or busyness, brokenness or apathy, we are too often consumed with the chaos life inevitably brings.

This is when Jesus' invitation to come to Him and experience rest is so important. I love the Message's paraphrase of Matthew 11:28-30:

> *"Are you tired? Worn out? Burned out on religion? Come to me. Get away with me and you'll recover your life. I'll show you how to take a real rest. Walk with me and work with me—watch how I do it. Learn the unforced rhythms of grace. I won't lay anything heavy or ill-fitting on you. Keep company with me and you'll learn to live freely and lightly."*

31 Days to Coming Alive helps us "learn the unforced rhythms of grace."

4

Through *Coming Alive* you will be pleasantly surprised by how accessible Jesus really is.

In *Coming Alive* you'll be invited in by a hilarious or heartfelt story, shaped by the Word of God, and challenged to live this Truth out in your everyday life.

And by the time you finish *Coming Alive*, you'll feel like you've gained a trusted friend who has met with you every morning for 31 days to share her stories and invite Jesus to be a part of yours.

Now go grab a cup of coffee, jump in, and get ready to come alive!

Chris Jessen, Lead Pastor
Two Rivers Church, Chattanooga TN

An Invitation to Come Alive

It was a Saturday morning and we had flooded our small airport with people. I could see it in the eyes of the airport security guards—they were not sure if they should join our large group and enter into the revival we were having right there by the security gates, or if they should view it as a terrorist threat. See, after I had finally convinced the sweet people at the check-in desk that there *was* a country called Nepal and they *could* get all the luggage I had there, this large group of friends and family circled around me to pray me off. The small airport was filled with people of big faith who were sending me on the most stretching faith journey my legs had taken yet.

God had called me to leave everyone and everything I knew and loved, and settle on the opposite corner of the world to serve Him. They prayed me off, and God hugged me tight as I hugged everyone goodbye. What I knew as I walked through those gates was that while I was walking into a wild journey away from all of my earthly comforts, I was also walking hand-in-hand with the only One who can truly comfort—Jesus Christ.

I am not typically the crying type. Fast forward a few weeks after that airport departure, though, and you'd find a different woman. I had been crying every single night about the smallest of things. I had never felt so lonely or so lost. I guess I had assumed that since I had left everything to serve the God I love, that I would instantly love where He had called me to serve. That was not the case.

The truth was, it was hard. I missed the comforts of home. I missed my dear friends and family. I missed electricity that worked all the time. I missed hot water. I missed knowing how to do things—I had to become like a child again, learning things as if for the first time. On top of all of this, I had also just received news after being in Nepal for three weeks that my grandmother had passed away. I did not even know how to tell my newfound Nepalese friends why I was crying at church that day—I did not speak enough of the language to explain. I was lonely, afraid and desperate. I was desperate for the God I said I believed in to show up and show me Himself. And on one of those crying nights, He did.

If I take the wings of the morning and dwell in the uttermost parts of the sea, even then your hand shall lead me, even there your right hand shall hold me. Psalms 139:9

I had read that verse a thousand times before, but that night God breathed it right into my soul. It was dark that night. Dark in my house because the power was out (again!). Dark in my soul. Yet God promised me He was there.

Even the darkness is not dark to me, for the night is as bright as the day. For darkness is light with you. Psalms 139:12

Something else happened that night.

God spoke to my heart these simple words that have shaped and changed my life.

Come Alive.

Come Alive Jenn. I am a God that is Alive. In fact I am the only God that is truly alive. I overcame death to come alive and bring life.

When He had received the sour wine he said, "It is finished" and he bowed his head and gave up his spirit. John 19:30

But it did not end there!

If you continue to read in John 20 it shares how Jesus was dead, buried and then *rose again*! Our God is alive and He speaks living and active words to us.

For the Word of God is living and active... Hebrews 4:12a

God began to take me on a journey that night to accept his invitation to come alive in Christ daily—minute by minute, hour by hour. Here is where you come in. I want you to take that journey with me. In the Nepalese culture, I was surrounded by people worshipping idols all around me— dead, false gods who would never be able to interact with those worshipping them. When we accept the invitation of Christ to receive His forgiveness of our sins, we are also receiving an invitation to live alive in Christ.

It is so easy to get lost in the mundane of life. Let's be honest here, life gets busy. We can quickly slip into survival mode before we even blink.

We can easily get lost in the nine to five. In paying bills. In the things that make us comfortable. In trying to find the perfect mate. In trying to be the perfect church girl. In trying to finish a goal. In trying to figure out a goal. In trying to make sense of a messy broken family situation. In trying to be super mom, super wife, super friend (or super husband if you are a male!). In making a casserole every time there is one needed and making sure it looks like something Martha Stewart herself would serve. We get lost and in the process of life and we deaden our soul.

Come alive and Come awake. What an invitation.

I have come that they may have life and have it ABUNDANTLY.
John 10:10

Awake O sleeper and arise from the dead and Christ will shine on you.
Ephesians 5:14

God began to teach me how to come alive and live alive in the midst of the mundane. In the midst of the good times and the bad. I began to find God in the secular everyday moments, which turned them into sacred moments.

Would you be willing to take the steps of faith on a journey to coming alive? Let's grab a cup of coffee, grab the hand of Jesus, and *come alive!*

DAY 1: COMING ALIVE—IN CHRIST

I am a series of awkward events. I mean it. The craziest things happen to me all the time. In fact, as I typed that sentence so many situations came to mind that I had to take a break and just laugh at the memories that came flooding in. I want to invite you into one of those moments with me.

When I was a freshman in college, I took one of those orientation classes you are required to take. The college I attended was small, so at least this story doesn't involve one of those auditorium-style classrooms packed with hundreds of students. However, it was a room that had three levels with chairs in its own small auditorium-type way. I decided to sit on the top level, so I walked up to the top level, trying to give off the "I am a cool college kid now" vibe. I went to sit down in my chair and did not realize there was a malfunction with one of the chair legs. So as I sat down, the chair fell straight to the ground—with me, my book, and my cool, new college backpack making quite the not-so-cool scene. The scene escalated when the chair, the backpack , and I all tumbled down from the top level to the next level—on top of another chair, which belonged to a poor, unsuspecting student. Then, gaining momentum, my backpack, the broken chair, that other student who I had not even had a chance to introduce myself to, their chair and I all tumbled down the bottom level. It's only God's mercy that this was the last level. We tumbled onto another student who luckily had noticed what was happening and had braced for the impact. It took the teacher and several other helpful students to dig us out.

Welcome to freshman orientation class.

Ok, you can quit laughing now and journey with me to my spiritual point. The malfunction of the chair occurred at the most important part—the base. It was impossible to sit in that chair, because it was broken at the point that is built to hold the chair up.

We can only come alive if we start with the most important foundation—Christ Jesus. It's only in Christ Jesus that we find life. He is all that holds us up.

Check out John 10:10. What does it have to say about Jesus's offer of life to us? He came that we might have *abundant life.*

Let me ask you, have you come alive spiritually by asking Christ Jesus to be your Lord? Romans 6:23 says that "the wages of sin is death, but the free gift of God is eternal life in Christ Jesus our Lord." The truth is, we all make mistakes called sin that cause us to be unworthy of a relationship with our perfect, Holy, sinless God. We deserve no relationship with Him. But He wanted us to have eternal life available to us—so He sent His precious son, John 3:16 style, to die, so we could experience spiritual life. That's glory shouting stuff right there.

It's amazing how simple it is to accept the invitation of Jesus. Romans 10:9 says "Because if you confess with your mouth that Jesus is Lord and believe in your heart that God raised Him from the dead, then you will be saved."

What an awesome promise packed in two little words: confess and believe. Friend, if you have not already, please open and accept your invitation to come alive in Christ. When you do, please tell others so they can celebrate with you. This calls for a big Jesus party.

If you have been a Christian for seven years or seventy years, would you take a moment and remember the life transforming truth that we have a relationship with a Savior, who died for us, and rose again? Sometimes it can become so "normal", especially if you have grown up in church since you were in the nursery being rocked by Sister Pat (well, at least that was who rocked me). Don't miss the power in the fact that you are in relationship with a risen Savior.

He's alive.

Therefore, you and I can live alive in Christ—no longer weighed down, dead in our sins.

10

Heart work:

Take some time to remember when you opened your invitation to accept Christ into your heart and life. How did you hear His invitation? If you have not accepted Him, and you are ready, take the time now to confess and believe that He is Lord, risen from the dead, and the Savior of your sins.

Read John 3:16 as if you are reading it for the first time. What impact does that have on your heart?
For the creative ones among us, have some fun. Make a fancy invitation from Jesus to you, where He invites you to LIFE.

Read Matthew 27-28. These chapters hold the power-packed story of Jesus's death, burial and resurrection. How does this story of death to life encourage you to live alive?

DAY TWO: COME AWAY

What does it do to your heart to think about a vacation? Where would you go right now if you could get away to your favorite place in the world—to get away from the mundane and come away to peace, rest and fun? Find that happy place in your mind; close your eyes and picture it.

If you have a journal with you, take a second and journal about that place. The sights and sounds and smells that come to you when you close your eyes.

So many places come to my mind. I love to hike in the mountains, although I am not one of those outdoorsy girls who have the right hiking backpacks and such. I am just a poser. I love the beach. I do not like the whole bathing suit at the beach thing, but I love the sounds of the waves, the feel of the sand, and sitting in the beach chair. I love traveling worldwide—from a monastery I stayed at for a free vacation (that's a story I will have to tell you sometime) in South Carolina to Tokyo, Japan.

The thing about a vacation is you get to come away from your normal. You set out for something different, to slow down (or if you go to Disneyworld, speed up!) and enjoy.

And oftentimes on a vacation you come away with people. You take someone with you. Usually it is family or friends (I mean, I guess you could take a complete stranger, but that would be strange) that you choose to come away with you.

Hand Family vacations were always filled with some sort of crazy disaster, like the engine of the truck pulling the camper literally blowing up hundreds of miles away from home. These vacations may have had many disasters, but they were also full of memories made together—laughing together, playing together, and weathering the disasters together. Riding from Tennessee to Niagara Falls in Canada under a camper top with bolted Suburu brat seats in the back of a pickup truck together. Coming away and coming together.

What if I told you one of the first steps to coming alive is to come away?

What if you heard the Lord whisper this to your soul,

Arise my love, my beautiful one, and come away,
For behold the winter is past, the rain is over and gone.
The flowers appear on the earth the time of singing has come.
Song of Solomon 2:10

Jesus longs for you to come away with him. He set the example. He used to go away with His father. He would take time out of the busyness of healing the sick, feeding the masses, and teaching His disciples, to retreat and commune with His Father. In Matthew 14:22, we are told of Jesus withdrawing by himself on the mountain to pray. So I guess Jesus was a mountain man. He must have liked the beach also, because he spent a great deal of time on the water. Not sure how He felt about bathing suits.

See, it sounds simple—to come alive, we must come away. If you grew up in church, you heard about doing your daily quiet time. If you are new to this Christian thing, you may have no idea what a quiet time even is. If you and I get really honest, sometimes it seems so overwhelming, so dry. So, how can I carve out thirty minutes in my day to sit still before the Lord?

I like to refer to it more as a come away time then a quiet time. Often, it's not quiet with me. I sometimes giggle with God when I am pouring my heart to Him in prayer. I come away with Him and praise Him with loud singing in the shower. It's not possible to take a vacation every day. However, it is possible to come away with the King every day. It's as simple as talking to Him. Eyes opened or closed, it doesn't matter (as long as you aren't driving of course). Sitting, standing, kneeling, running, swimming, horseback riding while talking to him, you are still coming away!

The God that created our universe, that breathed the stars into place, wants to speak with you, with me. He calls us "friend".

I have called you friends. John 15:15

Wow. Let that penetrate deep into your heart. He has called you friend. When you come away with Him, making a point to talk with Him, listen for Him just like you would for your friends. He will respond, He will speak. Just like some of my favorite vacations involved some of my best friends—coming away with the King is coming away with a friend.

His word is written as a love letter to you, full of the whole story of His plans for the world and for you.

For some people, finding time to come away to come alive means having to set the alarm clock at 5:30 am (gulp). For others it may mean during your kiddo's nap time, or between changing diapers and cleaning spilled glue out of the carpet. For others, it is late at night when everyone is asleep. But let me remind you, it's stealing away for moments with the King all day. While driving, while studying, in a conversation with a great friend—invite the Lord there with you, notice Him because He is already there.

As you come away, find the way that works the best for you. For me, it involves coffee, picking my favorite coffee mug for the day, good worship music playing, a nice juicy pen and a pretty journal. For you it may be looking for the perfect spot to sit outside. Jesus made us all unique and different in what makes us come alive as we come away. Find a good study. Ask people to help. Do not let the Bible overwhelm you and cause you to stay away because you feel you do not know enough, or understand enough. Get a great devotional. Get a great friend to help you. Be bold. Be risky. But come away.

14

Heart work:

What does it do in your heart to know God is inviting you to come away with Him

What can you do to move towards coming away with Him more?

Read John 15. As you read it, think about the personal relationship God wants to have with you. Make it personal. Re-write it with your name in it. (ex: verse 8—Just as the Father has loved me I have loved you Jenn, abide in my love.)

Day Three: Come Alive in the Common

It is easy to stay caught up in the commonness of our lives. We get used to the routine of things. We get used to having a to-do list and doing whatever it takes to get those tasks done. I am not a to-do list kind of girl. If I wrote one, I would probably quickly forget where I put it, or in the middle of writing it get distracted and forget to finish it. However, I do know it is very easy to get caught up in life and forget to come alive.

Recently, I was driving home on a country road when I noticed the truck in front of me suddenly stopped. I was shocked to see what happened next. These men were grinning from ear to ear as they jumped out of the truck and went to grab something on the side of the road. Let your imagination run as you picture it with me. They went to grab a fat dead stinky skunk. Yes, they stopped everything to excitedly pick up a dead piece of road kill. I have no idea what they were going to do with Mr. Flattened Skunk, and honestly, I am not sure I want to know! The point is they intentionally stopped what they were doing in their day to go after something dead.

I long to spend my days stopping to celebrate what is alive.

But if the Spirit of Him who raised Jesus from the dead dwells in you, He who raised Christ Jesus from the dead will also give life to your mortal bodies

Through His Spirit who indwells you.
Romans 8:11

The Greek word for life in that verse is *zooopeio* (how is that for a party of a word?), and it means to make alive, to vivify. When I studied the definition of vivify it means to give life, animate, quicken.

If you have accepted Christ's invitation to forgiveness, you get another gift—The Holy Spirit coming to dwell inside of you. Recognizing that gift alone can bring life to even the most mundane and common day.

God longs to commune with us in the common. Jesus used common things like bread and fish to feed thousands. He used common fisherman doing their common fisherman duties. In fact John 21:1-11 tells the story of Jesus coming to these fisherman in their ordinary day as they did their ordinary work. I imagine how those fisherman's hearts were coming alive as they pulled in so many fish that their nets were breaking. Communing with Jesus in the common brought an extraordinary joy.

Communing with Jesus in our common keeps our hearts alive. Talk to Jesus as you do that sink full of dirty dishes.

Sing your heart out to Jesus in the shower. Well, as long as whoever you live with doesn't mind. I just recently moved to another apartment and got a roommate after living alone for the past year and half. I realized one morning maybe I should tone down my coming alive in the common shower worshipping singing at the top of my lungs, so that my poor roommate didn't have to wear sound canceling headphones.

Take a walk with Jesus. Have a coffee date with Him in the morning. Invite him to sit with you and your four year old as you build yet another lego tower, just to see it quickly knocked down.

The seven dwarfs whistled while they worked. When you invite Christ into your common, you worship while you work.

It changes me. It changes the view of my day from mundane to majesty.

There is another amazing benefit. As I commune with Jesus in the common it reminds me that I am not common. You are not common. It may seem that the things you do in your day are unknown and unnoticed, but they are seen. You are seen.

Behold the eye of the Lord is on those who fear Him. Psalms 33:18

Come alive by communing with Christ in your common today.

Heart work:

Write out what your typical day looks like. What is your schedule? What feels like the most common, ordinary parts of your day? Now get creative. Ask the Lord to show you how He wants to enter into even your most common.

Read 1 Samuel 16:1-13. How did God break into David's common?

Read John 21 and the story of Jesus breaking into the disciples' common.

At the end of your day reflect on how you saw Christ in your common moments.

Day Four: Coming Alive in Creation

I don't know how I feel about the flies buzzing around me right now. I could do without them, to be honest. Their buzzing is distracting and I may or may not have just told one of them to flee from me in the name of Jesus (ok, I didn't say it as dramatically as that). I am finding the birds hilarious though. I am typing on my back porch—well really it's a stoop, but I like the idea of a porch much better, so in my mind it's a porch.

I live in a duplex, and the lady who lives above me has bird feeders on her porch. Those birds are happily eating away at the bird buffet. However, they crack open the seeds and are spitting out what they don't eat. Those chewed-up-and-spit-out seeds keep falling on my head. I find it oddly amusing.

The landlord is currently cutting my grass. It's beautiful. I appreciate green lush grass. I posted on Facebook that if there were a scent of perfume that was cut grass I would wear it. Several friends posted back where I could buy perfume scented like grass. It was at that moment that I realized I was not super serious about smelling like a lawn.

Romans 1:20 tells us that God's invisible attributes, mainly his eternal power and divine nature, have been clearly perceived, ever since the creation of the world, in all things that have been made.

So we can perceive things about God through the things He has made.

Our God truly is a creative , colorful, vibrant, powerful God. God could have made the world in black and white, but He filled it with so many shades of color.

God could have made one common animal, but Genesis describes how He made varieties of animals, plants, ecosystems, environments, even the land and the sea. The powerful part of God? He spoke all of creation into being with His words.

Just let that sink in. Look outside at creation. Think about how our God creatively, artistically spoke creation into being. Then I want you to pause. Really pause. Pause from whatever else you are thinking about and realize that the same God that spoke creation into being, speaks to you.

The same God that planned the universe, planned you.

So when you worship the God of creation you can worship the God who is creating a story for you.

Every day, there is a beautiful sunrise and sunset. The same vibrant hand of God that positioned the sun to paint the sunrise and sunset is painting a picture in your life.

I admit, there are many days I am not up early enough to see the sunrise. I do faithfully set my alarm at 6:00 every morning and I pretty much faithfully push snooze enough times until my clock says, I am turning off. And I wonder, if you like me, forget to notice the sunsets most days. But when you do—wow—the beautiful colors can take your breath away.

Notice the paintbrush of God today. What variety. What bold strokes. What tiny details, like the petals of a flower. God is writing a glory story.

And God said, "Let there be light", and there was light. Genesis 1:3

These powerful words flung light into a place that was void and dark.

God's word can fling light into places in our hearts that feel void and dark. Out of darkness and into glory.

I lift up my eyes to the hills, from where does my help come?
My help comes from the Lord who made heaven and earth.
Psalms 121:1-2

Our help today comes from the God of creation who made heaven and earth.

He will help walk you towards holiness, wholeness, and healing on those days when your soul needs rest. He will be your help when you feel helpless. He will pour out His presence when you need peace.

Think of the tallest mountain you have ever seen. I have had the joy of flying over Mt. Everest on a mountain flight. I thought I was in trouble when the stewardess said the pilot wanted to see me in the cockpit. My heart was thumping hard in my chest with a mixture of motion sickness as the tiny plane lurched, and my wondering what rule I had broken that the pilot wanted to see me. What I did not know is they invite everyone on that plane into the cockpit for the pilot to point out the majestic top of Mount Everest.

That mountain top that I was looking at, from an airplane, high above even where the eagles soar—that mountain was spoken into place by God.

I will lift up my eyes to the hills, where does my help come from? From the God who is able to make and move mountains.

Come alive as you look at creation today, knowing that the God who created the heavens and earth is creating His story in you.

Heart work:

Think about your favorite place in creation. What does it look like? Write about or think about the details in that place. The bold strokes and the tiny detailed ones. Praise the God of creation who painted that scene.

Read Psalms 121. Where do you feel you need some "soul help" right now. Place your name in these verses. Read them slowly. Ask the Lord to help you look to Him for your help to come from.

Read Genesis 1 thinking about our creative God. Do something creative if that makes you come alive. Go out in creation if that makes you come alive. But as you pause and think about creation, think about the creative story God is writing in your life – the beautiful portrait He is painting.

Day Five: Come Alive by Constant Prayer

1 Thessalonians 5:16-17 says, "Rejoice always, pray without ceasing." Does anyone else read that and feel slightly overwhelmed? Without ceasing. Those are the words that sometimes trip me up.

Without ceasing means a process that never ceases. No stop, no finish point. No coming to an end.

Reading this verse and understanding the definition of "without ceasing" has the potential to make us feel like a failure pretty quickly. It can seem unobtainable to make our lives a continual "Dear Lord…" without the "Amen".

I am a talker. In seventh grade, on the way home from a long van ride from Memphis to Chattanooga Tennessee, my youth minister at the time made a bet with me. Now, having been a chaperone many times on youth events, I understand this bet more than ever before. Jimmy, my youth minister, bet me that I could not keep silent for the entire van ride home. It was his way of keeping his sanity, not having to listen to my endless seventh grade girl chatter.

It sounded like an easy bet that I felt sure I would win. However about ten minutes into the bet, I realized this was going to be hard. So I decided to make it easier and go to sleep. I shut my eyes and went to sleep. This was a great plan, except that when I woke up hours later, I had forgotten about the bet.

I woke up talking. Therefore, I lost. (Although I should admit that I was supposed to clean his office for winning the bet, and I still have yet to perform my end of the deal).

The enemy longs for us to see prayer as a burden, a chore, something we are never going to be good enough at. Do you ever hear the whisper that your words are not eloquent enough for prayer?

Laying your head down on the pillow at night, do you ever stop and realize that the busyness and chaos of your day did not cease, but your prayers did?

When we have a relationship with God through belief in His son Jesus Christ, we have opportunity to have unbroken unending conversation with Him. Prayer truly is a sweet gift. It's whispering the secret depths of our heart to the greatest secret keeper.

It's communicating with him about our chaos, our desires, our joys, our sorrows.

It's trading our worries for His wisdom, our pain for His peace, our confusion for His confidence.

This was according to the eternal purpose that he has realized in Christ Jesus our Lord, in whom we have boldness and access with confidence through our faith in him. Ephesians 3:11-12

Drawing near with confidence to the throne of grace comes with conversation with him.

Prayers vocalized and prayers from the quiet depths of your heart. Prayers whispered and prayers that you may want to shout; each are conversations with the King.

The story of Esther in the Bible is a fascinating one. It's full of some fun girly stuff like beauty treatments and queens. It also has wild parties sprinkled in, tales of attempted murder and other various excitement. Esther, a simple Jewish girl, ends up becoming the queen for the king. Esther had a big request she needed to bring before the king—she needed to know if He would save her people. But she could only approach the King if He extended his golden scepter to her.

The good news: The king did extend his golden scepter, which resulted in deliverance for the people. (Esther 8). The good news for us-- our King has extended the golden scepter as well. He extended a cross on a hill that stretched from heaven to earth, bridging the gap of sin with a Savior.

He extends His nail pierced hand and offers a chance to come into the chambers of the King through prayer. It does

24

not have to be complicated. It is constantly inviting the King of glory in.

The prayer of a righteous person has great power as it is working.
James 1:16

Heart work:

Read the story of Esther and her approaching the king in Esther chapter 8. Imagine what it was like to be in that position, and the king extend his scepter to hear her request. Now think about how the king of heaven and earth has extended the invitation to hear your heart's request. What will you ask Him?

Read and reflect on Ephesians 3 as a reminder of the character of Christ. How does it encourage you to come alive in prayer?

Day Six: Coming Alive in Confident Prayer

One of my favorite things is to listen to my little nephew pray. His prayers make me giggle, and sometimes make me teary eyed all in the same blessing of the meal prayer. Alex got in his four year old mind one Christmas that he wanted a Power Wheels Jeep. He began to use his prayer time as an opportunity to remind God (and His parents) that He desired this gift more than anything for Christmas.

He would confidently approach God with a prayer like this, "God, thank you for the Power Wheels I am going to get at Christmas." Then He would tell His parents He was going to get a Power Wheels Jeep that cost thirty-five dollars. I am not sure where He got that number in his mind, but that was what he determined and prayed for.

I don't know if you have looked at the going price for Power Wheels in your spare time lately, but they are way more than thirty-five dollars.

My sister and her husband decided they would look around for a Power Wheels just in case. Guess what? They found one for exactly thirty-five dollars and were able to give it to Alex for Christmas!

He confidently exclaimed, "I knew God would answer my prayer."

Praise is due to you O God and to you vows shall be performed, O you who hear prayer. Psalms 65:1-2

Stop and ponder that.

The God of the universe hears our prayers. Just now, reading that sentence, I got so excited I almost spilled my coffee all over the table at Panera.

God heard my nephew's four-year-old prayer. God hears the prayer of the college student desperately wanting to avoid temptation. God hears the prayers of a loved one watching a family member suffer in the hospital. God hears the prayers of the pastor's wife praying for her husband as He ministers to a church. God hears the prayers of the stay at home mom who just wants a nap. God hears the prayers of the one who needs a job, the one who hates their job, the one who just has no idea how to perform well at their job. God hears the prayers of the husband wanting to provide for his family. God hears your prayers.

Prayer truly is a sweet gift. It's whispering the secret depths of our heart to the greatest secret keeper. It's communicating with him about our chaos, our desires, our joys, our sorrows.

And we can do it with confidence.

Let us then with confidence draw near to the throne of grace
That we might receive mercy and find grace to help us in time of need.
Hebrews 4:16

I think often fear keeps us back from praying with bold confidence. At least it does for me. It can be scary to pray specific prayers, because what if God does not answer the way we expect?

What if God at the core of His character is not really good? That's what Satan, the father of lies, would love for us to believe. So we pray safe, generic prayers, instead of powerful, specific prayers based on the promises of God.

I love this quote from Kelly Minter in her book on Nehemiah. "Do you shy away from prayer because of a lack of trust or intimacy with God? Do you feel safer keeping things in your own hands and under your control?" Ouch. That's the sound of my toes being stepped on a bit.

Recently, I have learned about pressing in and praying specific prayers, asking Him to do the big miracle of healing my Dad from his rare aggressive form of leukemia. Honestly, it was scary to pray specific please heal my Dad prayers.

What if God did not? What would that mean for my prayer life, my view of God, my relationship with Him?

But the Bible is full of promises that God is healer. Like this one from Jeremiah 17:14, *"Heal me oh Lord and I shall be healed."* Could I lean in and pray that promise like this? *Lord, Heal my Dad and He should be healed, because you are a God who can heal. That is Your character. That is Your power. That is a possibility.*

With shaky confidence I did. I prayed the promises of God. This week my Dad's doctor handed him a scripture card with that very same verse written on it, plus my Dad's bone marrow biopsy results. Those results? They said 0.0000 trace of leukemia. Healed. Gone. Glory.

I was glad that I prayed the promises of God so when God answered, I was confident it was Him. That is what praying with confidence does. It means that even if God does not answer the way I expected, when I see an answer, I know it is Him. That He is faithful. That He is divinely orchestrating a story. And that He is who He says He is.

So why not pray in confidence, with specific requests, specific desires, and specific questions? Then we can take God's specific promises from His word. Even if God surprises us with His answer, we can confidently know it was Him fulfilling those specific requests, desires and answering those specific questions.

Heart work:

What was the last specific answer to a specific prayer you received from God? Journal with thanksgiving how the Lord gave you that answer.

Read about Hannah's specific soul pouring out prayer time in 1 Samuel Chapter 1 and 2. Chapter 1, verse 15 mentions Hannah pouring out her soul before the Lord. What is one part of your heart you have been afraid to pour out before the Lord in prayer?

Would you be willing to take a step of faith and let a friend know how they can be praying for you? And then ask them how you can pray for them.

DAY 7: COMING ALIVE IN WAITING

How do you feel about waiting? Picture waiting in line. Close your eyes and imagine you are waiting in line at the DMV to renew your driver's license. I pick that because I think I waited in that line one time so long that by the time I got to the clerk, I had aged another year and I was not having very Christian-like thoughts. I imagine that when you imagine waiting in the DMV line you are not picturing yourself twirling around and dancing with joy because you love waiting in line. Nope. I imagine just the thought of waiting in a long line may or may not make you want to break out in hives.

We are a people who do not enjoy waiting. It's easy to want something and want it now. We're a fast-food society. *Welcome to McDonalds can I take your order?* (True confession—I love McDonald's dollar menu!) However, the truth is, all of us must wait for something at some point in time. So, if we do not like waiting, then how do we come alive in the waiting?

The first thing to do is to think about what you are waiting for. Maybe you are waiting for a new job, or to finish school, or to find the love of your life? Are you waiting for a phone call with results of a medical test? Are you waiting to see an answer to a prayer you have been praying for days, months or years?

Maybe you are waiting for simple things like for the buzzer to go off for the brownies you are baking, or waiting for your friend to arrive at your coffee date, or waiting for your husband to get home from work and distract the kiddos so you can make dinner.

Regardless of what you are waiting for, you and I are often waiting for something.

Coming alive in waiting? That seems impossible.

I imagine the Israelites grew tired of waiting for the Promised Land at times. In fact, those were some grumbling people. We probably would have been grumblers too. Imagine camping out with thousands of your closest friends, every moment of the day and night. And picking up and moving often, on your journey to the Promised Land—a land that you had not seen yet.

Promised, yet not yet experienced or seen.

In waiting, it can feel dangerous to hope, to expect, to dream—to risk.

Numbers 21 tells the story of the Isrealites getting impatient. Verse 4 of this chapter states, *"And the people became impatient on the way. And the people spoke against God and against Moses, 'Why have you brought us up out of Egypt to die in the wilderness? For there is no food and there is no water and we loathe this worthless food.'"*

Have you ever felt like you were going to die in the wilderness of waiting?

The truth is, as believer, we are ultimately in the waiting. We are waiting for the fulfillment of the promise of heaven. We are in the here-and-now, created with restless pangs of longing for the promised-yet-not-experienced.

In my Father's house are many rooms. If it were not so, would I have told you that I go to prepare a place for you? John 14:2

When you accept the invitation of Jesus Christ, you are accepting the promise of a place with Him in heaven. A place not yet experienced, but promised.

What if we press into the restless longings that waiting brings?

Psalms 37:4 says, *"Be still before the Lord and wait patiently for him."* When you study the Hebrew meaning of this phrase "wait patiently", part of the definition states to dance, to twirl, to whirl.

I like the idea of dancing in the waiting.

Every night when I was a little girl, when my Dad would come home from work we would dance. All day, I would look forward to that moment when my Daddy would come home and I would step my tiny feet on his not-so-tiny feet, he would hum the music, and we would dance. The truth is, my feet are bigger now, but I still love to step on my Daddy's feet and dance.

What if the waiting can become dancing with our Father God? Putting our feet on His and trusting Him to teach us the steps, the rhythm, the movement? Trusting Him to be our partner and lead us? When I was in dance class in college, the instructor was constantly telling me to let the man lead. What if we trust God's lead? His timing—even when it does not seem to fit our own; His steps—even when they are different then the ones we had planned.

Heart work:

What do you feel you are waiting on right now? How do you think the Lord wants to keep your heart alive in the waiting room?

Read Psalms 37:3-7, Psalms 62:1, Isaiah 30:15, and Lamentations 3:26. How do these verses speak to coming alive in waiting?

2 Corinthians 5:1-9 discusses the longing and hope for heaven, and how that effects our walking by faith and not by sight. How is God calling you to walk in faith in the waiting in your own life?

DAY EIGHT: COMING ALIVE CLEAN

I have a weakness for massages. I love them. This is an impractical love in America, as massages are not quite in the budget. However, when I lived overseas, massages were very inexpensive, and I fully took advantage of that oh so wonderful gift from the Lord. I also have a huge weakness for coffee. I will never forget the time in Nepal where my love for massage and coffee got me into a hilarious situation. One weekend we were staying at a fancy hotel for a team retreat, which had an attached spa.

Granted, I could not afford this kind of thing in America, but in Nepal, it was affordable. So the spa with the sauna and hot tub were calling my name. On my way, I saw the "spa menu" and I could not resist a peek. On the spa menu I saw a coffee massage.

In my mind, I immediately saw heaven come down to earth with a vision of getting a back massage while sipping coffee. I signed up faster than you could say Mahima (glory in Nepalese). This sweet little Nepalese woman walked in and I was in for a surprise. This sweet little Nepalese lady took coffee beans that were ground up and began to scrub and scrub. She scrubbed so hard I am pretty sure my legs caught on fire. I think they sparked and started the coffee grounds boiling! There was nothing fun about this process at all. How could I have ever thought that combining my two favorite things—coffee and massage would ever be a good idea? She coated my whole body in these coffee grounds, poured hot water all over, wrapped me in Saran Wrap and left me to brew!

I could not stop laughing during the twenty minutes when they left me there. I just paid money to brew myself like a cup of strong coffee. I felt like I deserved a t-shirt that said "I've been scrubbed clean, I've been coffee-beaned!"

Psalm 51 is a beautiful Psalm written by David in which David pours out his heart before God, asking God for a clean heart.

Create in me a clean heart O God and renew a right spirit within me. Cast me not away from your presence and take not your Holy Spirit from me. Psalm 51:10

David was face to face with sin in his life, and he wanted his heart to be purified, to be made clean. The stains of adultery and murder were leaving permanent dirt on his heart.

After my "spa treatment", I looked up the coffee scrub on the internet. I wanted to find out if this was a real thing— or just a crazy practical joke that had been played on me. I found out that coffee scrubs are a beautifying treatment. They are designed to scrub off all the dead skin, leaving fresh new skin. I do not doubt that it scrubbed a layer of skin off, but the process was not so fun.

Our hearts can be the same way. Like David in Psalm 51, we have layers around our heart that need to be purified, scrubbed off. Maybe it is the lies of Satan that we have believed for so long that it has silenced the truth of God. Maybe it is an addiction that clouds our heart, keeping us from feeling the freedom of coming alive with a clean heart.

Maybe it is a wall of fear or despair, anger or bitterness, jealousy or selfishness.

Maybe jealously of a friend has clouded your heart. Maybe bitterness is holding you in bondage. Maybe you find yourself compromising. Maybe it's gossiping about the other ladies at church in the form of a prayer request. Maybe it's a heart consumed with doubt in God. We all have areas of sin and bondage that need to be cleansed from our heart.

Our God's spiritual health and beauty spa specializes in our heart. From the youngest to the oldest, from the one who has walked with the God the closest to the one who feels far away—we all need God to lovingly create in us a clean heart.

Not only are we promised a new heart, we are promised a new self. Ephesians 4:23-24 tells us to, *"put on the new self, created after the likeness of God in true righteousness and holiness."* The old must be removed for the new to be revealed. We must be purified and scrubbed clean by the nail-scarred hands that bled for you and me. We all need God to lovingly create in us a clean heart. Our God is the God who promises in Lamentations 3:23 that His mercies are new every morning.

Are you ready to enter God's beauty spa? You've been scrubbed clean—you've been redeemed!

Heart work:

Read Psalm 51. Imagine God coming in to do a scrub on your heart. Confess the old that you would like to be scrubbed away. What areas of your heart are you afraid for Him to see? Romans 8:1 reminds us that, *"there is therefore now no condemnation for those in Christ Jesus."* Praise him for new righteousness and holiness!

Read 2 Corinthians 7:1. Write a prayer of praise for the ways God is bringing His holiness to completion in you as he cleans your heart

DAY NINE: COMING ALIVE IN CONFIDENCE

Have you ever thrown away something of importance to you? Then had that moment when you realized you would do anything to get it back—including digging in the trashcan? I remember in high school getting that dreaded thing called a retainer. Really, hadn't our teeth already been through enough with those metal torture devices called braces?

When my sister and I got these brand new retainers to keep our teeth straight, our parents repeatedly gave us the "Do NOT Throw These Away" speeches. So one week after getting them we went away to summer youth camp. The look on my sister's face was one of true panic at dinner one night when she realized she had left that very important retainer on her tray, which had gone down the conveyor belt and into the trash can. Faster than you can imagine, she was at that very trash can, digging through everyone else's mess, trying to find her retainer. Unfortunately, she did not find her retainer and had to make the call to tell my parents that she had lost it.

Therefore now, do not throw away your confidence which has a great reward. Hebrews 10: 35

I don't know about you, but for me it's so easy to throw away my confidence before I realize what I have done. Like that retainer on that tray, I can throw away my confidence in who I am in Christ, right into Satan's trash can.
Your friend points out how you have failed them in your friendship—you feel guilty and like you can never be a good friend again.

You are surrounded by people at the gym who have the body type that you can only imagine having—you feel like you do not belong, so you do not go back.

You step out in shaky fear and do something outside of your comfort zone – and when the fears come you throw away your confidence and return to a place that feels safe.

Satan loves when we throw away our confidence. He longs for us to shrink back. Hebrews 10:39 gives us a powerful charge.

We are not of those who shrink back and are destroyed but are of those who have faith and preserve the soul.

Let's not shrink back. What if we became those who walked into a room, confident in who we are in Christ? Not confident in our ability to do things perfectly, not confident in being the most beautiful, the most put together, or the most outstanding, but confident in the fact that we are wrapped up and covered by the Lord and His plan, power and presence in our lives. Do you have any idea how long and wide and high is the love that Christ has for you (Ephesians 3:18)? Wrap yourselves up in that and rest. Rest that you stand uncondemned (Romans 8:1).

You are fought for. You are rescued out of darkness into light because you are delighted in (Psalms 18:4-19).

You rest in the shelter of His wings (Psalms 91:1) The God of the angel armies is fighting for you (Ephesians 6:10-12). The times you feel you are in the desert, God will provide for you, protect you, and position you towards the promised land.

He is the God who parts even the most difficult red sea and provides a way for you to walk across (Joshua 2:10)

He is—and you are His (Isaiah 43:1).

He is the bread of life and he can turn five loaves and 2 fish into a feast with leftovers for a take home box (Mark 8:1-8).

This is the God that you stand confident in. This is how we can keep from throwing away our confidence—throwing back the truth of God's word at the things that try to cause us to shrink back.

Heart work:

Re-read the verses that were listed above. Pick several and pray them as promises over areas where you are feeling ready to shrink back from God-fidence.

What are some areas in your life you are feeling unconfident in right now? Pray and take these thoughts to the God who longs to pour out His power and presence in you.

Reflect over a "red sea" moment where God has surprised you with His miraculous power.

DAY TEN: COMING ALIVE IN FEAR
By TJ Ellis

Today I have the joy of introducing you to my dear friend TJ Ellis. She is a faith hero to me, and one of the most amazing faithful prayer warriors I know. TJ and I had the joy of meeting in high school when I was her "tutor" and helped her take notes in class, as TJ has cerebral palsy and is only able to have limited mobility of her hand. TJ may live in a physical body tied to a wheelchair, but her spiritual life soars. I want to share with you in the next two days devotionals she has written on TJ's blog, www.writingforhisglory.blogspot.com. She is an incredible writer and I know you are going to be so blessed.

When I was younger, almost the only thing I ever got in trouble for was talking back to my mom. I discovered this week that there is something that we should talk back to. Various situations that have come up this week have evoked great fear in me. It is not just one particular incident, but several. Fear is something I continue to battle on a regular basis. It may be fear of not succeeding, or fear or a conflict never being resolved. Sometimes my fear is that I will never change for the better. I fear struggling with the same things, but never having the courage or the means to change things. Most of all, I'm afraid to continue in fear.

It occurred to me, what if I were to talk back to my fears using God's truth? To be honest, I find this easier said then done. To do this will require both mental and practical effort on my part. Do you challenge your fear, or do you agree with it?

I envy people who by nature are not fearful. I often beat myself up wondering what is wrong with me? Why do I allow myself to be fearful? What can I do to stop it? Honestly for me, there are only two weapons that have put a dent in my fear. One of these weapons is filling my mind with God's words. I would love to be able to tell you that at this point I am doing a great job at that. The truth is, if I were to be graded this week, I would not pass the test. I have been reminded today that the great reality about God is that unlike people, or unlike me, God's patience does not run out. He does not keep a record of how many times I've tripped over the same obstacle.

I want to boldly refute my fears. I want you to boldly refute your fears. When you recite God's truth about fear, the fear does become less. Pouring out my fears is helpful for me instead of simply ignoring these and hoping these go away. Fear may not be something you wrestle with, however I'm still confident that whatever your struggle, whether it is physical, emotional or spiritual—or all of the above this promise is worth making your own.

"Fear not for I am with you; be not dismayed for I am your God; I will strengthen you, I will help you, I will uphold you with my righteous right hand." Isaiah 41:10

The I in this verse refers to God, and what He is faithful to do. I am reminded that while this battle is bigger then me, it is not bigger then God.

Heart work:

Write out a few of your fears. Now boldly refute them as TJ encourages us to do with some truth from God's word about fear.

Look up online or in Bible concordance the word fear: Write out some of the verses that stuck most to your heart.

Read 1 John 4:18. How does fear look in the face of His perfect love?

DAY 11: COMING ALIVE IN DISAPPOINTMENT

By TJ Ellis

Do you remember your first major disappointment in life? That baseball game you did not win or that birthday you were sick? We do not have to live long before we discover that disappointment is an inevitable part of life. As we get older, the disappointment we experience somehow seems more crucial.

We might not get the job we dreamed of, or the clean bill of health we expected from the doctor. As hard as we might try, we cannot exempt ourselves from the pain of disappointment. So do we just need to pretend that we are not disappointed? I have tried that and it does not work too well.

Do we just learn to cope or get over it? I guess in some situations that might work, but what about when that does not work for us?

And hope does not put us to shame, because God's love has been poured into our hearts through the Holy Spirit, who has been given to us.
Romans 5:5

This verse has become such a source of comfort for me, as I pray it will for you. As a Christian, our ultimate hope is the gospel. People and circumstances will disappoint us. There will be hopes and dreams in this life that may remain unfulfilled. However, there is a hope that will not fail us. When God promises us unending hope in His Son, He delivers.

He does not disappoint us. If we are disappointed, it is because we misunderstand God's nature or ways. If we are disappointed with God, the problem is not with God, but our limited, finite perspective and lack of understanding.

We do not see the big picture or the full scope of things in life. By simple trust, we rest in hope that far surpasses our greatest expectations. We can hold tightly to a hope that cannot be taken from us!

It is refreshing to know that when situations in our lives crumble, we can still rest in a hope that cannot be shaken. According to this verse, not only do believers have a continuous hope but we also have an outpouring of God's love into our hearts through the Holy Spirit.

What a miraculous transaction of God's perfect abundant love into our hearts! A limitless love. What a beautiful picture——Can you imagine the living God pouring His love into your heart? This is better than the pouring of iced tea into an empty cup.

Our souls are empty without the limitless love of Christ, and a hope that never falters, despite shaky circumstances, limited perspective, and unreliable emotions. That outpouring of love is more then just a supernatural high, but brings comfort, and is intended to be shared with others. The more we pour out God's love upon others, as He pours it in, the more we will be refilled with that ever satisfying hope and consuming love. Our hearts cannot hold the depth of such love in total fullness.

Heart work:

Is there a verse or truth from God's word that brings you comfort in times of disappointment or chaos?

What does Romans 5:5 mean to your heart as you apply it to situations of disappointment in your life?

Read Ephesians 1:18-23. What hope does that bring to your heart?

42

DAY 12: COMING ALIVE IN THE DANCE

Have you ever been asked to dance? Does the thought of being asked to dance make your heart pitter patter? Or does the thought of being asked to dance bring back a memory to your mind? Maybe the memory of a favorite high school prom, or a homecoming dance where that hunk of a man (or at least that is what your high school mind at the time thought) came and asked you to dance? I'm sure it was probably not quite like in the movies where He sauntered over and said, "My lady may I have this dance?"

Well, it was probably more like, "Hey wanna dance?" Not quite so romantic sounding, but hey, at least He sauntered over right?

When I think of dancing, several memories come to mind. First of all, you should know that I am not a good dancer. This girl has no dance groove in her. There is no such thing as gracefully gliding across the floor for me. It is more of a *clump, clump, whoops!* kind of feeling. Maybe that is why I was so good at clogging as a kid. Ballet was not for me. So my mom decided we would try clogging. I know it's not the most popular dancing style. But I loved it. My sister and I clogged for many years (even thought it was not really cool— I will be honest!) We had the big red and white checkered dresses that poofed out much further than our little chicken legs. But we had a great time doing it. Play us a little "Good Ol' RockyTop" and we could clog away. However, after elementary school we realized how un-cool this form of dancing was, and we quit. It is a very rare person that has seen me clog in a long while, but I found when the right music comes on, I still have it in me!

I will never forget the time in Nepal when I was asked to dance. I walked into a large conference area, where there happened to be a Hindu wedding going on. I just happened to show up right at that time. I walked into the room and heard over the loudspeaker, "And here comes our American dancer." In seemingly one movement, all of the hundreds of Nepalese people at this wedding turn and look with expectant faces towards me. Their eyes found mine and I am sure that wondered why I looked so stunned. I looked right and looked left, looking for the "American dancer". I realized with a deep sinking feeling in my stomach that I was the only white girl in a sea of brown faces, no other American looking person to be found. I thought to myself, *surely I heard them wrong.*

Then I heard it again. "And here comes the American dancer!" Wild applause followed and then I found myself being led towards to center of the room by the hand of a perfect stranger. Keep in mind that I knew none of these people. And unfortunately for them, what they did not know is that I am no American dancer! They were probably expecting Brittany Spears (she is their idea of America) and they did not realize they were getting Barely Steps Without Falling Instead. The crowd gathered around and they told me to start dancing. What do you do when you are suddenly placed in the spotlight of hundreds of perfect strangers and you really have no idea how to dance, especially not to Hindi music?

You do the only dance that you can remember from those horrible middle school dances, the Electric Slide.

I know what you are thinking, *Jenn, does the Electric Slide really work as a dance to Hindi music?* Well, to be honest, no, but it is the first thing I could think of at the time. I looked and felt ridiculous, but I did what they asked——I danced. And much to my surprise, even though my dance steps did not really look right, I had a great time.

Our lives are a dance. Most of the time, we may not really know what the exact steps are. The background music changes through the different stages of our lives. The type of dance changes. The pace of the dance steps are different, and sometimes the rhythm of the steps change before we know

44

what happens. But we have a dance partner who whispers to us, *My beloved if you will just focus on my face, I will guide your steps.*

If you look into my eyes you will see that I am confident in my steps and you can become more confident in yours. Jesus has called you to gaze. He has called you to gaze first into his eyes, and then He says, *Beloved, my I have this dance?*

How do I know this? Psalms 33:18 says, *"Behold the eye of the Lord is on those who fear him, on those who hope in His steadfast love."* One Chapter later, Psalms 34:5 promises that *"those who look to Him are radiant and their faces shall never be ashamed."* Jesus is looking at you; His eyes are on you. And if you will tilt your head upward, and let your eyes find his, your face shall never be ashamed. So what if you do not know the steps, or cannot keep the rhythm? What a promise to never feel ashamed. We spend so much of our lives stuck in shame. Satan loves for us to live that way.

Satan tells you to be ashamed of your body——that you will never be pretty enough, so just stay on the sidelines and do not dance. Satan tells you that you must be stuck in the shame of your childhood abuse, stuck in the shame of the hurtful words that were spoken over you. Satan tells you that you will never get the steps right, so why try? Satan tells you that you cannot trust your dance partner, so do not even think about dancing. But if we will just look into the loving gaze of the one who asked us to dance this thing called life, with Him taking the lead, our faces shall never be ashamed. Let the weight of the glory of that promise rest in your heart for a minute.

Psalms 30:11 says, *"You have turned for me my mourning into dancing, you have loosed my sackcloth and clothed me with gladness, that my glory my sing your praise and not be silent."* Ladies, it is time for us to become dancing women. We serve a God that turns our mourning into dancing! It does not mean we will not mourn, but we can mourn knowing that God will turn it into a dance, that our glory may sing his praise. Now that is a reason to dance. An extended nail-scarred hand gently lifts your chin up out of the muck and the mire of your circumstance. Out of the pain and the heartbreak. Out of the fear and the doubt. Out of the anger and the bitterness. Out of the seemingly unbreakable addiction. Out of the lonely nights and boring days. Out of the mundane and normal. Out of the crazy circumstances and the relationship that you just cannot figure out. Out of the sadness caused by shame. Out of the death-giving lies of Satan into the life giving truths of a Savior. Take the hand of the one who extends the invitation to dance. And once you take his hand, know that He will never leave you or forsake you.

I want to leave you with this poem. I am not usually much of a poet, but I believe God gave it to me so that I could give it to you.

Freedom Song

Abundant, Joy-filled, Dancing Life
Walking in all surpassing peace, lots of dancing for me
Dancing with the King of Kings.
He's extended His hand and asked me to dance
Not hidden and unseen, but truly known and loved
Asked to dance by the King of Kings.
No fear in the steps
No trying to keep up with the beat
Instead just stepping on His feet
Asked to dance by the King of Kings.
Why do you worry so much about trying to do it right?
Instead, look into His eyes, because you are precious in His
sight.
You were asked to dance by the King of Kings
You are His dancing Queen
Do not be afraid
Do not strive
Just dance with the King of Kings at your side

46

Heart work:

Journal about a few dance experiences that you have had in your life. What does the idea of dancing bring to your heart?

If you could pick any dance and any music to represent your heart, what would it be? Now picture yourself dancing with Jesus. What does that look like to you?

Read Psalms 30:11-12. How has God turned your mourning into dancing. How are you still in "sackcloths" and not quite clothed in joy yet? Say a prayer thinking God for what He has done, and asking Him for what else He needs to do!

Psalms 34:5-6 Imagine that you are gazing into the eyes of your savior. What do they look like? If you can draw or find some creative way to picture this, do. What does God see when He looks through His eyes at you?

DAY 13: COMING ALIVE IN DARKNESS

In Psalms 27, David pours out his heart before God and proclaims that even in the midst of a difficult battle, He will not be afraid, because He is pledging to make the Lord his ultimate confidence. The Lord that He knew he could cling to even in the darkest night. And David had experienced some dark nights. Some dark nights just tending sheep. Some of those dark nights I am sure were full of wondering. Thinking to himself, *"Um, I was anointed king right? So why am I still out here in this dark night tending sheep? Does not seem like the most kingly thing to do. My sheep companions may follow me, but I would not exactly call them my kingdom. If they are they sure are a stinky kingdom."*

There were some dark nights for David. But I love what Psalms 27:1 says. *"The Lord is my light and my salvation whom shall I fear?"*

I think most children have at least a little fear of the dark in them. I was never terrified of the dark, but I never went seeking it either. When I was a camp counselor, we had many kiddos that were scared of the dark. I could always tell the ones who were most afraid because they would stick to me like glue if we were hiking back on the path from the campfire to our cabin. Why? Because I was the light leader, the one with the flashlight.

The Christian life is a journey in which we celebrate walking in the light. We walk in the light but sometimes forget that we once were in darkness. In fact, we had to be rescued from the darkness. No matter if, like me, you were a young child when you accepted Christ and the worst sin you did was steal an extra cookie, or you were saved a year ago out of an addiction to drugs, the moment you accepted Christ you were rescued from darkness to light. Colossians 1:13 says, *"For He has delivered us from the domain of darkness and transferred us to the kingdom of His beloved Son."* Reading this should cause you to do a little praise party. Dance a happy jig; shout hallelujah! Remember that you were rescued by the ultimate knight-in-shining-armor who was determined not to let you live in the domain of darkness.

He fought all the forces of hell to come to you while you lived on earth. He came and said, *Trust me. Let me deliver you. No more darkness dwelling for you. Let me take you to a different kingdom. The kingdom where you have belonged all this time. The kingdom of light. But it is a journey. You will not go directly to the kingdom where there is no need of the light of the sun or the moon due to the light of my beloved Son. No, I cannot take you there right away. But as you are living on this kingdom called earth, I have transferred you in such a way where you can live with one foot in the kingdom called heaven. And I am never going to leave you on this journey. I sacrificed too much to rescue you. To deliver you.*

I am the light of the world; he who follows me shall not walk in the darkness but shall have the light of life! John 1:12

No matter what is trying to keep you in bondage today, do not feel powerless to the darkness. Ask God to help you remember the power found in the light. In the light there is liberation. In the light of God's truth, I stand free from any bondage Satan tries to keep in my life. If we are walking in the light we are liberated. Just because I am liberated does not mean there is not a battle. Liberation and freedom come through the battle. But if I am willing to take up the full armor of God and battle with His truth as my weapon, the darkness must flee!

Maybe you can be with me there, you can celebrate the fact that you were rescued out of sin, transferred from the kingdom of darkness into light.

Hold on. God's word is *"a lamp unto your feet and a light unto your path."* Psalms 119:105

Wait for the Lord; Be strong and let your heart take courage; Yes wait for the Lord! Psalms 27:14

Enjoy the light. Celebrate the light. Dance in the light. Sing in the light. Rejoice in the light.

Shine the light.

Heart work:

What is your testimony of being delivered from the darkness to the kingdom of light?

How did you celebrate the light today? Did you find yourself rejoicing in the light provided by Jesus, the light of your world?

Reflect on a time in your life when you wondered if you would ever find the light at the end of the tunnel? Journal through how that felt. How was God the light for you in the midst of that struggle? Praise the Father of light for being with you. Reflect over the glories that God did in that time.

Write Psalms 27 into a personal prayer for yourself.

How do you want God to liberate any of your present darkness?

DAY 14: COMING ALIVE CHOSEN

Take a moment and think back to elementary school. Now, true confession, I did not get to spend much time on the playground in elementary school. I was always in trouble for talking in class, and most of my recess days were spent on the wall in trouble. But if you remember recess days do you remember the game of red rover? *Red Rover, Red Rover, send <insert name here> right over.* I always got nervous during that game.

Would I be chosen? I wanted to be chosen in one way, because it meant my classmates knew my name, noticed me, thought of me. However, I did not to want to have to run right over and try to break through the arm chain my classmates had made. I imagine they may have outlawed that game on playgrounds now after one too many broken arms.

Then, there were sporting teams. I never seemed to be chosen for them. I was the girl they said should probably sit on the bench.

Then, you've got those middle school and high school years when you want to be chosen by the "in crowd". You want to be asked to the dance, be chosen by THAT boy, be noticed.

Then, when you become a "grown up" you want to be chosen for that job, that position, that title, that group at church.

We live a lot of our lives wanting, longing even, to be chosen. Being chosen means you are noticed, named, worth it, a somebody. The enemy of our souls spends a great deal of time whispering lies that say you are not chosen, named, or worth it; that you are a nobody.

Friends you **are** chosen. You are called by name. Like in Red Rover, Jesus has called you right over.

But now thus says the Lord, He who created you O Jacob, he who formed you O Israel. Fear not, for I have redeemed you, I have called you by name you are mine. Isaiah 43:1-2

In Old Testament times, the priests held the most important positions, because they connected the people to the presence of the Lord. They were specifically chosen, set apart. The Bible even describes them as clothed in beauty. Full of beauty (those priestly garments were fancy schmancy!), set apart, and chosen. They lived out their chosen lives helping people connect to the presence of the one who had chosen them.

Guess what?? When Jesus came to be your friend and chose you, called you by name—you are also clothed in His beauty, set apart, and chosen.

But you are a chosen race, a royal priesthood, a holy nation, a people for His own possession, that you may proclaim the excellencies of him who called you out of darkness into his marvelous light. 1 Peter 2:9

You can live out your chosen lives helping people connect to the one who has chosen you.

Chosen.

Yes. That's you. And me. No more waiting on the sidelines, feeling left out, wondering if you are known. You are chosen by the God of the universe, set apart for Him. You represent Christ to the people. Live out your day today coming alive as a chosen one.

Heart work:

Think back to a time when you felt left out, when you were not chosen for something. Then think about a time when you were chosen. Contrast those two experiences.

Read 1 Peter, Chapter 2. What does it mean for you to live out your life as a chosen priest, a living stone?

Read Isaiah 61:6 and put your name in it. You are a priest of the Lord.

Who can you be a priest to today, helping connect their hearts to the presence of God?

DAY 15: COME ALIVE BY EXPERIENCING MORE

There are days when it is easy to settle for mundane instead of more. When it feels easier to experience misery instead of majesty. We find ourselves molding into the pattern of the world instead of moving on with God.

When we accept Christ's invitation to come, we are also accepting an invitation to more. Our God is a more kind of God.

Ephesians 3:20 is a glorious promise for our lives. *"Now to Him who is able to do MORE abundantly then all we can ask or think, according to the power at work within us, and to him be glory in the church and in Christ Jesus throughout all generations, forever and ever amen."*

I like more. If I am eating ice cream, I usually want more. Same for chocolate cake, coffee, and french fries. Those "more's" usually leave me wishing I had experienced less. The "more" that God has for us is a more we can fully celebrate in freedom. His divine invitation to come alive includes an invitation to more.

Need more courage? More freedom? More peace? More joy? More wisdom?

The Bible is packed full of invitations for us to experience more of all of these things.

And the peace of God which surpasses all of your understanding will guard your hearts and minds in Christ Jesus. The kind of more peace that will surpass all of your understanding. Philippians 4:7

If any of you lacks wisdom let him ask God, who gives GENEROUSLY and without reproach and it will be given to him. The kind of more wisdom that is generous and lavish. These are great more words. James 1:5

Do you ever find yourself longing for more but living like most? We long for more but we limit ourselves to living like most everyone else. God has planted the longing for more in us because He wants us to believe Him to do more than we could ever ask or imagine.

Many times we miss our more because we look at most everyone else and turn what they have into a must. For example, most people are married by 27, so if I am still single I must be unloveable. Most people go to college, so I must or I am a failure. Most moms on Pinterest make their own detergent and perfect craft supplies so I must or I am a terrible mother.

What if we did not allow ourselves to turn our "mosts" into "musts"? What if we stopped feeling like "not enough"? What if we simply focus on God's more for us? Abraham and Sarah are good examples of a more, most and must story. In Abraham's day, most everyone had children. It was expected. You needed to have children to pass on an inheritance. Genesis 16 tells us how Sarai (before her name was changed to Sarah) was unable to have children like most everyone else. She was not sure she could trust in God's promise, so wanting to be like most, she took matters into her own hands and told Abraham to take a mistress. As you can imagine, this only ended in jealously and unfulfilled longing. This was not the "more" that God had in store for her. Genesis 17 and 21 share how God did have a "more" plan and how he fulfilled it.

Do not miss your "more" trying to be like most everyone else. God's ways are so much higher than we can ask or imagine. Come alive in your more.

Heart work:

Read Isaiah 55:8-9. What does it do for your heart today to know that God's ways are higher than your ways. Dream with God today about what your imaginations are. Then, praise Him that He has even more than that for you.

Read the most, must, more story of Abraham and Sarah in Gen 16, 17, 21. How can you apply that to your own life?

What are some more then you could ask or imagine things God has done in your life?

DAY 16: COMING ALIVE IN FREEDOM

There is something that just makes a girl panic when you feel trapped or stuck. I think back to some of my days as a camp counselor when we took the campers caving. I had to pretend that I enjoyed being in a small, dark cave under the earth, but the reality is that I did not really like the claustrophobic feeling that came with that.

Last week I was remembering how it felt to be trapped when I was doing some work on my car outside. Good old Toby the Taurus is a rebellious little car, so whenever I am going to be somewhere more than a day I have to unhook my battery so it will not drain and die. I went outside to hook my battery back up and had a "situation". I was wearing a scarf (there is that scarf again) and while hooking the battery up, the hood slammed shut on my scarf. The scarf was just deep enough in there that I was stuck. Trapped by a scarf and my car hood. (It's alright, you can laugh at me). I was stuck there for about twenty minutes until someone came to the duplex I live in and was able to pop the hood.

When there are things in life you long to be free from, sometimes it is easy to become overwhelmed and feel trapped. Trapped by a sin struggle, a relationship, a situation, a thought pattern, a fear. You want to wiggle your way out into freedom, but cannot seem to find the right key to unlock the door, or in my case, pop the hood of my car.

Galatians 5:1 is such a glorious promise that I cling to over and over again. *"It is for freedom that Christ has set me free. Stand firm therefore and do not be burdened again by a yoke of slavery."*

This is the most glorious truth in finding freedom. It is not outward things that set us free and keep us free, it is Christ in me!

Often in our fight for freedom we start with the outward things: following the right rules or looking for that list of outward things to do that will unlock the door to freedom. Then, when we miss a step, we begin to think we are paralyzed. That freedom may be for Suzy Q and John Doe Christian but not for us. What a difference it makes in the fight for freedom that it is not us fighting but Christ who has already fought for us!

We have a God who fought and broke the chains of death so we might experience life! Even as I wrote that I just had to let out a good old fashioned glory shout here at our kitchen table.

Death could not hold our Jesus down. Three days later he arose, he appeared, and he ascended into heaven to intercede for us. *It is for freedom that Christ has set us free.* Colossians 1:27 stuns me when it tells me that it is *"Christ in me, the hope of glory."* The hope of glory is that Christ is in me. In you. Christ in me sets me free and keeps me free.

The temptation as we look at that things we want to break free from is for the struggle to look so big and the freedom giver to begin to look small. We can come alive in freedom if we honestly look at the power of the freedom giver.

Little children, you are from God, and have overcome them, for he who is IN you is greater than he who is in the world. 1 John 4:4

There is power in that little word, "in". You are wrapped up in Christ and Christ is in you. Wow. The freedom fighter is the freedom giver. When you begin to feel chains of shame, sin, fear or failure trap you where you cannot seem to wiggle free, invite the freedom giver to come pop the hood of your heart and release you.

Heart work:

In what areas are you longing to experience freedom but feel trapped? Read Galatians 5:1. How can you stand firm in these areas and not be burdened again by a yoke of slavery as you think about Christ in you?

Read Ephesians 4:23. How is your new self created *in* Christ Jesus? The "in" changes what you put on.

Read James 1:20 and Ephesians 2:20. Where do you see the word "in" and how can that impact your longing for freedom?

DAY 17: COMING ALIVE IN THE NEW

Remember not the former things, nor consider the things of old. Behold I am doing a new thing, now it springs up, do you not perceive it? Isaiah 43:18

Living in the new is the adventure of saying yes to the now. However, it is so easy to stick with the old. We get comfortable in the old ways, old things, and sometimes even old lies that the enemy has told us.

I often shop at the thrift store. It is fun to find cheap old things and get use out of them. In fact, I love to buy blue jeans at the thrift store because they are already worn out, stretched out and lived in. They feel comfortable.

However, there is nothing like a new pair of jeans to make you feel like a supermodel. Well, at least if it is the right fitting pair of jeans.

Neither is new wine put into old wineskins. If it is, the skins burst and the wine is spilled and the skins are destroyed. But new wine is put into fresh wineskins and so both are preserved. Matthew 9:17

We can come alive looking for the new things God is doing. The new places God is leading. The new truths God is speaking to us—as we live in the now. Often, we miss the now because we are scared of the new. The old is comfortable. But what if we take the adventure of the new and now and let our hearts be like the new fresh wineskins mentioned in Matthew 9:17? Christ pouring the newness of His spirit into our fresh, moldable hearts daily. Living alive in the new things God is doing in the now.

Not looking back. Not clinging to the old shame. Not clinging to the old same. When I lived in Nepal I was terrified to begin to learn to drive. For good reason. There was no sense of traffic rules, they drove on the other side of the road , the random animals like giant cows wandered through the streets, and the people constantly crossing the road terrified me. However, I realized if I wanted to go anywhere I needed to get out of my comfort zone and learn to drive a scooter. I tried to convince myself that it really was just a big purple overgrown bicycle. I named my scooter, which I like to refer to as a motorcycle because it did have an engine, the purple pleasure. I was determined to learn to drive the purple pleasure. The old ways of having to take taxis everywhere would not get me where I needed to go. I needed to let go and learn the new.

I had my first few lessons and finally ventured out. And I loved it! It opened a whole new world to me. No more haggling with taxi drivers when they could clearly see I was a pushover. I could drive myself! For the most part, the driving worked out great, except for that one time I accidently ran over that duck's webbed foot and then had to watch it hobble around and plague me with guilt the rest of my time in Nepal.

There are times when coming alive in the new can seem to be very out of our comfort zone. Take this moment and be encouraged that the Lord Jesus Christ is doing a new thing in you. Our acceptance of Christ's invitation to our hearts is a new and now story.

Now if anyone is in Christ he is a new creation the old has gone the new has come. 2 Corinthians 5:17

I love that our Jesus brings the new into our lives. A caterpillar is simply a worm crawling on the ground in the dirt. Then it weaves a cocoon and goes into the chrysalis stage where through an amazing scientific process the caterpillar becomes a butterfly inside that cocoon. There in the darkness the worm develops wings. Once the worm gets wings, it is truly a new creation.

Christ transforms us into new creations. It is easy to forget at times that we are new. That we have wings. You are new. There are days the butterfly may not fly as high in the sky as other days, but the butterfly still has wings. It is physically impossible for the butterfly to go backwards and crawl on the ground in the dirt again.

You are new. Come alive in newness today.

Heart work:

What do you like about the idea of new? What scares you about "new things"?

What new things do you sense God is doing in your now?

Read Lamentations 3:23. Celebrate that His new mercies are a part of your now story.

Read Romans 6:4 and Romans 7:6.

DAY 18: COMING ALIVE IN SURPRISES

Sometimes in life we generally love when things surprise us. Tomorrow happens to be Valentine's Day, and I am sure there will be many hoping for a surprise gift from a loved one that says "Will you be mine?" Surprise gifts, surprise parties, a surprise check in the mail that you were not expecting—these things can make a person smile just thinking about them.

Not only is this week Valentine's Day, it has been a week which brought a fun surprise to us in southern Tennessee. It usually only snows a few snowflakes in the winter folks. This last week, the weathermen said it would snow and it really did. Not just a little, but a great deal of snow! For people without snowplows and four wheel drive, who really have never had a need for those things, the snow brought shut down and slow down to our lives. But it brought out the little child in us – the I-cannot-wait-to-build-a-snowman-and-throw-a-few-snowballs child in us. It was so much fun to go to bed and wake up the next day to a snow white, winter wonderland, transforming a our normal scene into a landscape that was postcard-worthy.

This was a surprise that broke into our everyday lives and changed our plans. Whatever people had planned for their days was changed. Sometimes, surprises that bring change in plans are good, while at other times surprises that bring change in plans are the kind that stop your heart and make you wonder if you will have to will it to beat again. The phone call with news you never wanted to hear, the relationship you did not expect to fall apart, the job that had to let you go.

When was the last time you experienced a surprise that brought with it a change in plans? Maybe it was a change in plans for the day, for the minute, for the next couple of hours, or even a change that would affect the rest of your life.

Regardless of what the surprise brings—good changes of plans like snowball fights and sledding—or changes of plans that seem to cause the ground beneath you to shake—let your soul take a rest in this truth. The God of surprises is the God who said let there be light, and there was. The Old Testament is full of God-sized surprises. The God who wanted the people of Israel to experience freedom and the promised land, so He parted the Red Sea. God shut the mouths of lions when Daniel was thrown in the lions den and used a stone and a slingshot and a young boy to knock down a giant named Goliath. The New Testament is also packed with God-shaped surprises. The God of surprises sent His son Jesus into the world and healed the sick, fed five thousand with a few loaves of bread and fish, and raised people from the dead. The God of surprises destroyed the plan of the enemy when Jesus was crucified, buried and rose again to surprise the guards guarding the tomb and the disciples grieving their goodbye.

We may be surprised, but God is not. Jeremiah 29:11 reminds us that, *"He knows the plans He has for you."* Surprises may seem to change things like our plans, our days, or our lives—but God does not change. We, as humans, change all the time. We change our minds about what we want for dinner, what we want to wear, what we want to be when we grow up. We change our minds about who and what we like and do not like. God does not change. He promises that.

Jesus Christ is the same yesterday today and forever. Hebrews 13:8 Every good and perfect gift is from above, coming down from the Father of lights, with whom there is no variation or shadow due to change. James 1: 17

Events in life may surprise us, God's plans may surprise us—but one thing that will never surprise us is the character of God. God will not wake up tomorrow, press snooze on his alarm and decide not to take care of the universe for the day. God will not decide he should not have sent His son to die and change His redemption plan. Our God does not change. Let His love surprise you today.

Heart work:

When was the last time you experienced a good surprise? What about one that did not feel as good?

How has the Lord surprised you with His love this day, this week, this year?

Read Jeremiah 29:11. Even if it is familiar to you place your name in it. In the gift of the knowing that God knows the plans He has for you.

DAY 19: COMING ALIVE IN STILLNESS

Stillness. Even just typing that word causes a breath of fresh air to enter my soul. A pause. A quietness. A pondering.

In the fast-paced, crazy world we live in today, it is hard to experience that word in our lives. That place where our bodies are still and quiet, where our minds are not racing in a million directions. Often, owe have so many places to be and so many things to do that it is hard not to forget where and when we are supposed to do them.

I will never forget the vacation I took to a monastery. I know most people do not look for monasteries to be their hopping vacation spot, but I was raising support be a missionary and had little in the way of finances. I found out you could stay at a monastery for a donation and so I said, "sign me up!" My sister and two other friends and I decided to give it a go and stay at a monastery in Charleston, South Carolina. It may not be the beach, but it was at least close to the beach. I loved my stay there. I may have scared the poor monks to death my first evening joining them as they ended their evening singing through the Psalms. It was a beautiful sound, one I will never forget. I imagine they never forgot the sound of me exiting the service that night either. I had no idea as I left they would sprinkle holy water on my forehead as a blessing. The room was dimly lit and the water blessing startled me. I let out an accidental scream then a laugh. My laughs are never quiet. I sure knew how to break the stillness.

On that "vacation", we were silent all through the day because we decided that would help us hear from the Lord. It was hard to be silent, to be still. It took a while for my brain and heart to quiet. When it did, it was amazing how I sensed the Lord speaking to my heart. Through his word, through walks in the woods, through the songs of the monks, through the stillness——He spoke.

66

Be. Still. Know. It is so easy to change what follows those words.

Be busy. Be perfect. Be supermom. Be the best Sunday school teacher. Be here, be there before you can be still. What if we stopped to experience stillness as a gift and a blessing in our everyday life? While you are at the stop light, pause, take a deep breath, thank God for that moment. Ask Him to still your heart. Ask Him to still your mind.

However you take your moment of stillness, revel in some awesome truths. Revel in the knowledge that God is preparing you, molding you, changing you, providing for you. He is washing you clean, pursuing you, loving you, holding you.

God is teaching you, meeting with you, covering you, wrapping you up in his arms. He is filling you, speaking through you, caring for you, touching you, healing you, giving you strength to mount up on wings like eagles (Isaiah 41:29-31).

God is opening the eyes of the blind, setting the captives free, making paupers into princesses. God is bringing hope to the hopeless. God is the potter you are the clay. God is actively working, mending, doing the extraordinary in the ordinary. God is reaching, loving, romancing, God is listening.

Be still and know. God is the *I am* so you do not have to be. So fall back, sit back, lean back into Him.

The more we KNOW what God is doing the easier it can become to allow our hearts and minds to be still. I think most all of you reading this are not monks living in a monastery who spend all your day focused on praise and prayer all day long. You are people with normal lives who sometimes go to bed too late and do not always wake up on time. I do not think that God is asking us to stop all that we are doing and just be still all the time. God may be calling you to stop some of what you are doing. Let Him whisper to you when you feel overextended what you may need to let go of.

But I do believe God's divine invitation to our hearts, our minds, our bodies is to let our souls magnify God by letting go of control and relaxing into what God is doing. Check out how the Message version states Psalms 46:8-10. *Attention, all! See the marvels of God! He plants flowers and trees all over the earth, Bans war from pole to pole, breaks all the weapons across his knee. "Step out of the traffic! Take a long, loving look at me, your High God, above politics, above everything."*

Friends, let's come alive today by taking a moment to step out of the traffic of our everyday lives and taking a long loving look at our God and His work in our lives.

Be still and know.

Heart work:

Set aside some time to find some stillness. Wherever and however that looks for you spend that stillness taking a loving look at God and His work in your lives.

I am going to leave the heart work at that. After all the work and the stillness do not go together.

DAY 20: COMING ALIVE AS GOD'S MASTERPIECE

Do you know that you are a masterpiece? You are God's masterpiece, in fact. Those are not just words on a page. Those are truths for you to fling back at the devil when he sneaks in with lies about who you are. If you google the definition of masterpiece, it comes up as a work of outstanding artistry, skill or workmanship.

God intricately designed you. Even your fingerprints are unique. I have an identical twin sister and even we are designed differently out of the same DNA. I have been known to have some confusing moments at times. Like the time I went with some friends in high school to our local aquarium. I was separated from my sister and the group of friends that she was walking around with. At one point I was excited when I saw her and I asked her if she was having a good time. When she did not respond I asked her again. She did not respond again. So I decided to playfully tap her and ask her why she was ignoring me. Imagine how foolish I felt when I realized I was talking to my reflection in a fish tank. Yes. You can laugh. I did. As did all the people around me that saw me do this.

As identical as my sister and I are, we are each a unique masterpiece carrying the fingerprints of our heavenly Father. Each person you encounter was uniquely crafted, designed and placed on this earth by God. To display His glory story.

There are many days when you and I may not feel like a masterpiece. We look in the mirror and wish that our artist had painted us differently. Ephesians 2:10 says, *"For you are His workmanship, created in Christ Jesus."* The fingers of God designed you. He knit you together.

It is easy to find ourselves focusing on the things that are not. I am not skinny enough, smart enough, strong enough, organized enough, funny enough and the list could go on and on. What if you walk into a room celebrating the gift of what you ARE? Now, this does not mean that we do not need to grow in areas of our lives where we are naturally not gifted. For example, Jesus skipped over the gift of organization and administration in me when He painted me with His paintbrush—this is an area I need to grow in. Like working out our physical bodies even when it requires moving muscles in new ways, we can work on those areas when we are weak. However, what if we experience life celebrating the way God created us versus spending energy mourning what we are not?

If you have children, I would bet some money on the fact that somewhere on your refrigerator is some piece of artwork that your child painted, scribbled, smeared, or cut and pasted for you. It may be identifiable or it may not. Regardless, your precious child made it. It is their masterpiece. You do not look at that piece of art and point out all the flaws, mistakes, ways it could have been better. If your five-year-old gives you a turkey made out of a handprint that looks more like a chicken or a buzzard, you proudly display it. He or she made it for you. You celebrate their workmanship.

God made you Psalms 139 style. He knit you together. You are fearfully and wonderfully made. He displays you for His glory. The same God who patterned the stars in the sky patterned you. Can you imagine what the world would be like if God simply took a man cookie cutter, and a woman cookie cutter—and formed us each the same? He is a creative God and He created you.

Are you an introvert? God celebrates the way He made you and how others come alive when you connect deeply with them one-on-one.

Are you an extrovert? God celebrates the way He made you to make a room full of people feel they are invited and included in your party.

Are you an athletic type? (Insert Jenn praying forgiveness for her jealousy here!) God celebrates the way He knit you together to be in action.

Are you a numbers person? God celebrates that ability to crunch those numbers into things that make sense. Celebrate, my friend. Enjoy your strengths. Ask God to help you with your weakness. In the process, walk into a room, a situation, a job, a place and walk in celebrating. Come alive in you—unique you. The comparison game will steal, kill and destroy the masterpiece He has made you to be.

Blessed be the Lord, the God of Israel, who alone does wondrous things. Blessed be His glorious name forever. Psalms 72:18

You, my friend, are one of God's wondrous things.

Heart work:

Start out this time by reading Psalms 139. Meditate on these verses.

Ask God to help you see some of the specific ways He fearfully and wonderfully made you. Make a list in your prayer journal and thank Him for these unique things about you.

This is going to be uncomfortable, but ask a close friend what they notice about how God made you. I imagine they celebrate things about you that you may not have even noticed.

DAY 21: COMING ALIVE LOVED

There is something that happens when a person falls in love. They get a different sparkle in their eye. They get that puppy love look. The "I cannot even say the name of the person I am falling in love with without blushing and a humongous smile on my face" look. It is easy to tell a person falling in love.

A person who is in love and knows they are loved walks around with the question of, " Am I loveable?" already answered. They know they are loved, therefore, the question is answered with a yes. Inside of our hearts lie questions like, "Am I loved?" and, "Am I worthy of love?", and " Will you love me"? Do you remember those notes that you passed to that boy in elementary school that said "Do you like me" Check yes or no!" It is almost like we have that inward note in our hearts and hand it to the people that we meet. Do you like me? Am I worthy of love?

When you live knowing you are loved, your heart comes alive. Love causes you to feel secure, important, noticed. Feeling loved makes you feel like someone took notice of you and liked what they saw. Feeling loved causes your heart to soar and your life to sing.

I do not know what your family is like. I am not sure if your family was one in which you felt loved, noticed, secure, or important. I do not know if you are in a relationship or marriage or have friendships that make you feel loved, noticed, secure or important. Regardless of if your circumstances are good or bad, I know that you are loved by someone. You are loved by the Savior Jesus Christ. You can stand secure in that.

Romans 8: 38-39 has a glory-shouting promise about God's love for us. *"For I am sure that neither death nor life, nor angels nor rulers, nor things present nor things to come, nor powers, nor height nor depth, nor anything else in all creation will be able to separate us from the love of God in Christ Jesus our Lord."*

There is nothing that does not fit into those categories there. God knew we would think there would be exceptions. Wrapped up in Jesus Christ, there are no exceptions. So get that huge smile and that sparkle in your eyes because you are loved!

Nothing will separate you from the love of God in Christ Jesus. That is promised security. John 3:16 reminds us that God loved the world (and that means you) so much that He sent His Son. To die. For you.

This love changes everything. Or it should. However, it is easy to forget how loved we are. Which makes it easy to sometimes unknowingly ask the people we come in contact with, "Do you like me?"

You are deeply loved. Let God whisper, shout, sing and dance this over you.

Beloved, I have declared that you are mine.
I called you by name. I looked across the portals of heaven and earth and I chose you.
Chocolates and flowers from an earthly lover are nice, but they are simply reflections of me, Jesus, the One who gave you my life.
So, beloved of mine, do not despair. If you feel unchosen, looked over, alone; this moment, remember:
I desire to take your heart and hand and twirl you around the room.
I have called you by name, you are mine, you are my divine design.
Look out today, I am sending love your way.
Check out the sunset, the reflection of my light.
Feel me in the hug of a friend so tight.
Enjoy dining with me—read my word and feast at a dinner fit for a queen.
You are not forgotten, looked over, or not enough,
You my precious—are loved.

Heart work:

God is love. Read 1 John 3:16. Then read 1 John 4:7-13. The Character of God is love.

How has God demonstrated His love to you?

Pick a Psalm or your favorite passage of Bible and write it as if it were a love letter written for you.

How does it change your life when you have the, "Am I loved" question answered?

DAY 22: COMING ALIVE IN THE CHARACTER OF GOD

We, as humans, are complex people. I have a Master's degree in counseling and the more I studied the more it was evident—people are complicated. We are made up of a complex system of body soul and spirit that sometimes works together and sometimes ends up in broken parts.

God's character is complex but not complicated. The character of God is hard to wrap our limited human minds around. Study the names of God in scripture and you can begin to see some of the amazing complexities to the character of God. You can find the qualities and characteristics of God wrapped up in the names used for God in scripture.

Imagine this scene with me. You are going about your daily business, walking outside, and all of the sudden a flame of fire bursts out of the shrubbery in front of you. The fire is there but the shrub is not burning up. Granted, I have been known to have a knack of accidently catching things on fire, but even for me this would be an odd, eye-catching experience. I am sure you, like me, would stop to see what was happening.

In Exodus Chapter 3, this happened to Moses. Even if you have grown up hearing this familiar passage, imagine what it would have been like to be there with Moses. What would you have done when the voice of the Lord started speaking out of that bush? I imagine I would have whipped off my flip flops to stand on that holy ground as fast as you could say fire. God had some big stuff to say to Moses. He was calling Moses to a task much bigger then himself. He was allowing Moses to enter into the passion of God to set His people free. The Israelites were in bondage to the Egyptians and God wanted to set them free. And God had chosen Moses to help.

Moses is stunned. I love what He said to God. He says in verse 13, *"if I say God has sent me to you, and they say what is His name, what do I say back to them?"*

Exodus 3:14 holds God's reply. *"And God said to Moses, 'I am who I am'. And He said, 'Say this to the people of Israel, 'I AM has sent me to you.'"*

God revealed His character as I am. He boils the complexity of His character down to one statement. I Am.

I am God.

I am He who was and is and is to come.

I am God and you do not have to be.

I am in control and you can let go.

I am moving, I am working, I am setting you free.

I am the Alpha and the Omega, the first and the last, the beginning and the end. Revelation 22:13

He wrote the story in the beginning, knows the end and has put us in the middle. We can come alive as a character in the story God has written because we can trust the character of God.

Like Moses did, what if you and I take off our shoes for a second and tread on Holy Ground? Celebrate the character of God. God is complex but not complicated. He boiled it down in that simple statement.

I am.

Heart work:

Read through the story of God calling Moses in Exodus 3. What do you sense God is calling you to do in His story?

Take a moment to think about areas in your life when you would feel in this statement.

I am not _____. Now contrast
that with God saying back to you, "But I Am."

Play Bible scholar for a second. Use a search engine on the
internet and look up names of God. Come alive as you see
those names the character of God.

Day 23: Coming Alive in Winter Seasons

I am not sure what season of year it is when you started this devotional. It is right smack dab in the winter as I am finishing up the writing journey for these pages. It has been a record winter for most of the United States. I have written much of these words under a warm blanket with a cup of coffee in hand. Granted, I would have had the coffee winter, spring, summer or fall. However, it has been a cold season.

In our lives, we go through seasons. Moments where we love the season we are in. Moments when we are ready to celebrate the turning of the days into a new season. I wonder if this day finds any of you who feel you are in a winter season in life? Maybe a time where things feel darker, colder, where it is hard to see growth. Can I encourage your heart today? If you feel stuck in winter, spring is coming. Eventually, you will see the bud of flowers breaking through the ground. The cold hard ground will thaw and the signs of new life will come.

It can be hard in the middle of a winter season of circumstances to hope for spring. Maybe it feels painful to hope, impossible, even. I remember my winter season last year. With my Father spending months and days and weeks at the hospital for cancer, and my sister and her family having a devastating accident, I wondered if spring would ever come.

Habakkuk may be a book in the Bible you are not very familiar with. I am going to have you feeling like quite the Biblical scholar today because you are going to read a verse from this little book that often is overlooked but is full of some powerful truths. Habakkuk was written during a rough season for Israel (then again there were many rough seasons). Habakkuk was a prophet who was basically asking God what are you doing, what is going on with your people, what is your plan here? Have you ever found yourself asking God those same questions? In winter seasons of your life—those times where the nights seem long and the growth seems frozen——you may have had those same questions on your heart. *God what are you doing in this situation? What is your plan here? I know your promise of Romans 8:28 working all things together for my good, but this is not appearing good.*

I love how Habakkuk begins to see God in this winter season. Habakkuk 3:17-19 , *"Though the fig tree should not blossom, nor fruit be on the vines, the produce of the live fail, and the fields yield no food, the flock be cut off from the fold, and there be no herd in the stalls, yet I will rejoice in the Lord; I will take joy in the God of my salvation. God the Lord, is my strength; he makes my feet like the deer's; he makes me tread on my high places."*

Now, do not read these verses and feel condemned, like you need to stuff your "I am sick of this winter season" emotions, and grin and bear it. Habakkuk came to this conclusion after some honest talks with God. In fact, the subtitle of Habakkuk 1 in my ESV study bible is "Habakkuk's Complaint". God wants you to come to Him with the struggle——with the good, the bad and the ugly. That is how we can come alive in seasons of winter.

In the cold winter there is nothing more comforting then to sit by a warm fire. There is something soothing about letting the flames of heat thaw you from your head to your toes. Hebrews 12:29 describes our God as a consuming fire. We can come into the presence of God with our hearts seemingly frozen in the darkness of winter and let Him slowly thaw our heart with his presence from our head to our toes. Ask Him to come into your winter. Ask Him to give you glimpses of spring. Ask him to grant you strength. And wait for Him to answer.

In the waiting time, can I give you permission to do something fun? Go out to eat with a friend. Take a bubble bath. Laugh. Cry. Watch a good movie. Go outside and play. Cook a new recipe. Light a candle. Use your good china——the kind that you save for special occasions. Read a new book.

Window shop in a fancy section of town. Do something you have always wanted to try but never taken the time. Hire a babysitter. Go on a date night with your husband. Have a girl's night in. If you are a man and happen to be reading this—grill something, play a video game, or hang out with some friends.

It does not really matter what it is. But I think one of the best ways to come alive in winter is to take a break and remember winter will eventually thaw. Take a moment as you have that fun and ask Jesus to continue to shine through your winter. To warm you in His presence in the midst. To give you peace, rest, strength, and joy .

Come alive by acknowledging your winter. Talk freely with the Lord about your struggle, your wonderings, your need for the light to shine. Pray, ponder and wait for the blooms of spring to push through. God will meet you in the winter.

Heart work:

Read through the book of Habakkuk. Try not to be intimidated. It's a short book. See how Habakkuk finds God in the "winter".

What is your fun thing that you are going to do? Write about how you came alive as you did it.

Ask someone to help pray you through your winter season. If you are not in a winter season currently you will be someday.

Write a prayer for when you do experience a hard season.

DAY 24: COMING ALIVE IN SPRING

Spring is full of new life. Flowers spring up from the ground that you may have forgotten you planted. Trees begin to become green again. There is a scent of newness in the air. Or, if you live in an area with lots of Bradford Pear trees like I do, a scent of pear tree dead fish odor in the air.

Song of Solomon describes spring in this way. Song of Solomon 2:10-13 says, *"Arise, my love, my beautiful one, and come away, for behold the winter is past; the rain is over and gone. The flowers appear on the earth, the time of singing has come, and the voice of the turtledove is heard in our land. The fig tree ripens its figs, and the vines are in blossom; they give forth fragrance. Arise, my love, my beautiful one, and come away."*

The winter is past. The season of singing has come. It is an incredible feeling when you have gone through a season of life that feels dark to experience that change of life season when the Lord says the winter is past. When I read these words it makes me want to break out into song. Pictures of the hills alive with the sound of music come to my mind! Spring is a gift from God that ushers in growth and new life.

John chapter 4 tells the story of a woman from Samaria. You may have heard her referred to as the woman at the well. This woman had been in a winter season in her life. She had her share of failed relationships. She'd had five husbands and was currently with a man who was not her husband. Shame followed her around her town. In fact, she was drawing water at a well at a different time of day from all the others. Though the day might have been sunny and hot, I wonder if she felt the winter in her soul. It had been a season of looking for love in all the wrong places, in addition to feeling constantly covered in a cloak of shame.

Enter Jesus. He came beside her at the well and asks her for some water. He then told her he could offer her living water, the kind that would quench her thirst forever. Eventually through the conversation, Jesus revealed to her that He was the Messiah. This woman's life was forever changed. Her winter suddenly turned to spring. She wanted everyone to celebrate the new life she had found. She immediately left her water jar (John 4:28) and told the people she had met a man who had told her everything she had ever done. She was walking in newness of life.

Behold the former things have come to pass, and new things I now declare. Isaiah 42:9

What new things is God speaking to your heart these days? Come alive as you take a moment and picture your story when you encountered Jesus. Spring sometimes brings stormy weather but even in the storms the signs of new life are everywhere. Every day that you walk in Christ you are a sign of newness of life.

We were buried therefore with him by baptism into death, in order that, just as Christ was raised from the dead by the glory of the Father, we too might walk in newness of life. Romans 6:4

Come alive today knowing that wrapped up in Christ you are walking in newness of life. The season of singing has come.

Zephaniah 3:17 describes a heavenly song——and guess what it involves? You. *The Lord your God is in your midst, a mighty one who will save; he will rejoice over you with gladness, he will quiet you by his love; he will exult over you with loud singing.*

Did you ever sing that little song as a child, "singing in the rain, just singing in the rain"? God is singing a melody of rejoicing over you. He is singing even in the rain. Let him quiet you with His love. Let it rain.

Heart work:

Since we talked about how the Lord is singing over you, would you take a moment to sing some praises back to Him? If you are in a place where it would be awkward to sing, like for example the Starbucks I am in right now, write out the words to your favorite praise song. Just take some time to praise Him.

Read the story of the woman at the well in John 4. How can you relate to this story?

What new things have you noticed Jesus speaking to your heart?

DAY 25: COMING ALIVE IN COMMUNITY

If you read the book of Acts, you will see the story of a community of believers running hard and fast after Jesus together. They were committed to spreading the life-changing story about the one who had changed their lives. It is a powerful story of a people together experiencing the power of Jesus. It was not always neat and tidy, but they were together. So together that Acts 2:44 says, *"And all who believed were together and had all things in common... and day by day, attending the temple together and breaking bread in their homes, they received their food with glad and generous hearts, praising God and having favor with the people."*

God puts a high value on community. Genesis 1:18 describes how females got on the scene. God said it was not good for man to be alone. In 1 Corinthians 12, the body of Christ is described, not as consisting of one member, but of many members. This passage goes on to describe the importance of each part of the body working together. The difficult struggle is that being in community with others is it is not always easy. The enemy loves to isolate us. Even in the midst of the struggle, coming alive in community with other believers is something worth fighting for. Authentic Christian community gets messy sometimes, but when the message is the center of the mess it magnifies the messiah and redemption comes.

When I lived overseas, our missionary community was one of the most beautiful pictures of the early church. We came from all different backgrounds, places, churches, but we all had one tie that bound us together. We had left our homes of comfort to serve the one who had called us to this country to share His name. We had a blast as a community together. Far away from our family and friends back home, we were knit together on the same battlefield of serving Jesus.

I remember our Thanksgiving celebrations as a community. My one friend Matt really wanted a turkey to eat as we celebrated Thanksgiving together. He was very excited when he found out he could have a turkey flown in from Australia. He got a price for this turkey but did not realize it was per kilogram, not just a flat fee. He had not one, but two turkeys flown in – and was shocked when he realized the price! It was too late for turning back, so he asked me if my teammate Leah and I would cook the turkey's for our feast. I had never cooked a turkey before, after all, that is a job for moms and grandmothers. However, I agreed. I have never been so nervous about cooking something before. After searching how to cook these turkeys, Leah and I went to work. We slathered it with lots and lots of butter (to hopefully cover any of our mistakes). Then I prayed over that bird so much I am pretty sure it was a Christian by the time we were done. Four different ovens later (our electricity kept going off) and several hours later, our thanksgiving feast was finished and we had a blast celebrating as a community.

What does your community look like? Have you found yourself isolating out of fear, hurt feelings, or lack of time to invest in community? Might I encourage you to run towards community? Run towards the community that is running with you towards the cross.

Authentic community is a safe place to kick up your feet on the coffee table and rest. Your community will be blessed when you take a risk and go into your community and offer them the authentic gift of you. Laugh together, pray together, mourn together and celebrate who God is together. The key word. Together.

And let us consider how to stir up one another to love and good works, not neglecting to meet together, as in the habit of some, but encouraging one another, and all the more as you see the day drawing near.
Hebrews 10:24-25

Christian community is made up of people who will make mistakes. There may be times your feelings will be hurt. There may be a time when you hurt someone's feelings. But don't give up. Don't give in. Don't miss the precious gift of community.

Celebrate what the early church had—believers loving each other so well in community that people wanted to know the Christ they formed their community around. Messy at times, but centered on the message of Jesus. Would you come alive in community today?

Heart work:

Read Acts 2:42-47 and Acts 4:32-37. How do these words describe Christian community?

Where do you find yourself in Christian community? Pray for this community. Thank God for this community. Ask God what you bring to this community.

How can you encourage someone in your community today? Pick one small thing to shower God's love on someone.

DAY 26: COMING ALIVE IN COURAGE

I must admit, I used to judge the disciple Peter. His story is found in Matthew 14. Here he was in a boat with a great deal of waves and wind, and they were having hard time getting the boat to shore. I cannot imagine being on that boat. I took a cruise and was sea sick on that giant cruise ship the entire time, and it was smooth water! So my stomach is lurching a bit with just the thought of being on a boat that windy evening. The disciples were interrupted from their panic, however, when they saw someone walking on the sea. Imagine their surprise when Jesus called out that it was him, just hanging out, walking on the waves.

Peter was bold. He told Jesus to ask him to come out on the water. I wonder if he really expected Jesus to say come. But Jesus did. He told Peter to come walk on the water. And guess what. Peter got out of the boat and did. The reason I judged Peter was because He got out on the water, took his eyes off Jesus and begin to sink. The super spiritual side of me thinks, "Come on Peter, you are looking into the eyes of Jesus, how could you be afraid and sink?"

Truth is, I should be cheering Peter on. If you notice, the rest of the disciples—they stayed in the boat. I would much rather be known as a follower of Christ who sinks versus one who stays in the boat and never gets the experience of walking out on the water. Peter had courage. He looked at where he was in the boat. He looked at where Jesus was calling him to come. He got out of the boat. He walked on water. Well, for a short time at least. He quickly lost focus on the safety found in the eyes of the Savior who had called him to come.

It is easy in life to lose our focus on the security available to us when we don't keep our eyes on the Savior inviting us to come. The waves loom large. The bills big. The circumstance impossible. The goal unattainable. The friendship seems unfixable. The ministry God called you to undoable. The situation seems to swallow you up and your faith motor does not seem to be working.

I will never forget the time that my Dad, sister and I got the crazy idea to go fishing on a big lake in a tiny boat. It was basically a rowboat with a motor attached. We were in a fishing slew when I heard a loud splash and saw bubbles all around our boat. We quickly realized the motor had fallen off the back of the boat into the deep water never to be found. This is not convenient when you are far away from the dock in a small boat. It is especially inconvenient when you have my sister's and my rowing skills! We rowed in circles again and again. Finally, my Dad was able to flag down a big boat which was willing to tie us to them and tow us back to the dock. The waves were big but it did not matter because we were secured to the bigger boat.

When your faith motor has died and you feel like drowning, remember that faith is not the absence of fear, but taking your fears to the Father. Faith is believing in the darkness what God has shown you in the light.

Hebrews 11 describes faith as an assurance of things hoped for, things not seen. Fear brings the opportunity to press deeply into the gift of faith, therefore gaining assurance. When our little boat was tied to the big boat, we were able to get to shore even without a motor. Faith is the chord of hope that ties us to the one who can take us across the waves back to the shore. Faith brings courage and causes us to do crazy things like get out of the boat and walk on the water.

Think about what Jesus is calling to you in this moment. Is He saying "Come"? What adventures is He inviting you into? What impossible are you in the middle of needing to see Him make possible?

Would you, like Peter, get out of the boat and walk on the water? Come alive in courage today, friend.

88

Heart work:

Read Joshua, Chapter 1. This is a passage where Joshua is taking on a pretty big God-sized job. In particular, focus on Joshua 1:6 and Joshua 1:9.

Where does your heart need courage today? Ask God to come in and give you the kind of faith that brings courage.

In what particular areas is Jesus calling you, like Peter, to get out of the boat and walk on the water?

DAY 27: COME ALIVE IN THANKFULNESS

Last week, my incredible pastor, Chris Jessen, sent an e-mail to our church planting leadership team. In the e-mail he encouraged us to pause and be thankful. As we did this, He challenged us to write out some things we were thankful for. This seems like such a simple exercise. The truth, though, is that it is a powerful weapon! We e-mailed each other the list of the things we were thankful for. It brought such joy to my heart as I read the responses. The wide variety of things each of us had to be thankful for. From the mundane things to God manifesting His presence in our lives, we had much to be thankful for. Big things, small things, in between things—thankful for the scope of all these things.

Philippians 4:6 gives us a charge that seems big but the reality is that it simply starts small. It says , *"Do not be anxious about anything, but in everything by prayer and supplication with thanksgiving let your requests be known to God."* It seems big to try to be anxious for nothing. But the small step is beginning with thanksgiving.

So, I want you to do your heart work now, right here in the middle of this devotional. Get a piece of paper, or your phone, or a stick to scribble in the dirt. Make a list. What do you have to thank God for? Start with some small things. Some tiny details of your life. For example, I am thankful for the warm fuzzy socks I have on my feet right now, a Starbucks gift card, the flowers a friend sent me, and a hot bath. Moving on to bigger things, I am thankful for the laughter of my niece and nephew, my car that runs most of the time, a warm house, God's provision for my daily needs, my family, and living out my God-sized dream. Even MORE, I am thankful for forgiveness of sin, the hope of eternity, miracles of healing, and God's spirit speaking through His word.

I wonder if a bit of the weight of the world lifted from your shoulders as you paused to give thanks. We do not mean to forget to have thankful hearts, but we get busy. We get bored. We get caught up in our lives and it is easy to forget the powerful gift of thankfulness.

Psalms 95:2 says, *"Let us come into his presence with thanksgiving, let us make a joyful noise to him with songs of praise."* Thanksgiving can usher us into the presence of God. David was called a man after God's own heart. Many of the Psalms written by him are full of thanksgiving. There are many other emotions throughout the book of Psalms, but thanksgiving is one of its beautiful themes.

I will praise the name of God with a song, I will magnify him with thanksgiving. Psalms 69:30

What an awesome gift. We can magnify the Lord with the simple task of offering thanks.

DAY 28 COMING ALIVE IN CONVICTION

My cute little nephew Alex has me figured out. As a matter of fact, so does my niece, who is only 18 months old. They both have figured out that I take my role as an aunt seriously. As an aunt, they know that I really cannot say no.

Can I have a donut at 9:00 at night Aunt Nenn? Why yes of course you can.

Can you stop what you are doing and take us to the playground Aunt Nenn? Of course—let's go!

My little niece knows she is as cute as a baby doll, so all she has to do is say please and I say yes. I can only remember really raising my voice at my nephew once. My sister and her husband and I were at the zoo in our little town. Alex has always been a small skinny little kiddo. My sister and her husband were looking at one of the animal exhibits, and Alex was right beside me. All of the sudden, I looked around and Alex had slipped away from me. I sure did raise my voice when I realize Alex had slipped his small little body in a hole in the fence surrounding the world's largest rodent exhibit. I could not let my little nephew be eaten by the world's largest rodent on my watch.

Picture a large human sized rat. Eating my nephew.

So I yelled, and I yelled loud. *"Get out of that cage Alex Michael Humbert."* It was a time to use his full name and get him out fast.

When you picture God, what do you picture? I have talked with lots of Christians and each one may answer that question in a unique way. One thing I have noticed is we tend to put human qualities on our infinite God.

If you had an angry absent Father, you may view God as an angry uninvolved father.

If you were hurt deeply in a relationship, you may tend to view God as someone who will hurt you.

If you grew up trying to be perfect, you may feel God equates perfection with being loveable.

The enemy gets excited when our view of God is warped. He throws a happy dance when we get stuck in our sins. We become afraid, buried underneath the weight of condemnation, unable to experience the freedom that comes with conviction.

Romans 8:1 There is therefore now no condemnation for those who are in Christ Jesus. For the law of the Spirit of life has set you free from the law of sin and death.

There is a difference between condemnation and conviction.

The voice of the Lord, wrapped in a love that died for our sins, convicts.

The voice of the enemy condemns.

The conviction of the Lord springs out of His longing for you to be free. Safe. Whole.

When I yelled at my nephew, it was out of a desire for him to be free. Safe. Whole. I called his full name and reached in and got him out of there.

When God speaks to our sin, it is out of a desire for us to be free. Safe. Whole. And Holy.

Condemnation says: *you are defined by your sin, you cannot be loved because of your sin, you are worthless because of your sin.*

Conviction from the Holy Spirit says: *you can be free and redeemed from your sin, you are already loved, and you are of great enough worth that I sent my son to set you free from your sin.*

Isaiah 43:1 I have called you by name, you are mine.

Sometimes the Lord has to call your full name. He may even do it loudly, to get your attention. To set you free from the cage of sin that can destroy you.

He is calling your name in love. Come alive when you experience the Lord's conviction. It can be in a sermon, your time reading the word, a conversation with a friend. Come alive knowing as the Lord brings conviction, He is loving you towards freedom and holiness.

Heart work:

How would you explain the difference between condemnation and conviction? Apply this to areas in your heart where you have felt the Lord convict you of certain areas of sin. How is this different from condemnation?

John 3:16 is a very familiar scripture, but check out John 3:18. What does this verse have to say about condemnation?

Listening to the voice of conviction ushers in freedom while condemnation can lead to feeling frozen in sin. Ask the Holy Spirit to bring conviction to your heart. Listen to what He says. Ask Him to free you from feel condemnation—which brings shame.

DAY 29 COMING ALIVE WHOLE

I love a good donut. One of my particular favorites is the pancakes and bacon donut at Julie Darling Donuts in downtown Chattanooga. A donut with maple syrup and bacon. Heaven. Jesus and I will eat those in heaven together someday——calorie free . I knew my love for this donut was becoming a problem when I would walk in and they instantly knew that's what I wanted. They even knew to heat it up for about ten seconds. My name is Jennifer and I have a donut problem.

The obvious thing about a donut is that that it has a hole in it. Well, unless it is a donut taken up a notch and filled with jelly or crème. Your typical donut, however, has a hole.

Imagine with me for a second (is your mouth watering yet) that you were kind enough to share this donut. So you broke the donut in half and handed one half to the person next to you. You must have been feeling very loving and Christ-like that day.

What if you did this and then you and your friend decided you wanted to make a whole donut again. I know it sounds silly, but picture it with me. There is no way you could take those two donuts and make it a whole donut again. Why? Because two halves do not make a whole.

We were created to long for God. We have a God shaped hole in our hearts that can only find wholeness when filled by the Holy one. God delights for our deepest desires to be filled in him. The challenge is that often we look for earthly temporal things to fill the holes in our heart.

We take our broken half and look for someone or something's broken half to complete us and make us whole.

That relationship will fill my hole.

That person's approval will fill my hole.

That job will fill my hole.

That new home, new thing, new outfit, new experience will fill my hole.

It will take my broken half and make me whole.

Insert Jesus, the Holy One. He wants to satisfy our deepest desires with the depths of His love. He is the half that completes us and makes us whole. That makes me want to shout glory.

He fulfills the desire of those who fear him; he also hears their cry and saves them. Psalms 145:19

The author of our desires fulfills our desires.

For He satisfies the longing soul, and the hungry soul He fills with good things. Psalms 107:9

What if you and I take our hungry souls and let him fill us to overflowing with Himself.

Heart work:

What do you find yourself looking for to fulfill deep longings in your heart? What are your go-to comforts when you experience a deep longing?

Read Ephesians 3:19 . What do you think it means to be filled with all the fullness of God?

How have you experienced the Lord's love filling you and make you whole? Celebrate that for a moment.

Day 30 Coming Alive in your Can't

By TJ Ellis

The sun was beaming down on the back of my neck. It would be like any other vacation. Or at least THOUGHT it would. We had only been in Panama City Florida two or three days before the "big event".

It was time to cross the sidewalk that separated the condo we were staying in from the beach. My mom asked my cousin to help me get over the sidewalk the correct way. Reaching for the controller on my wheelchair, I pushed his hand back. I informed him I could do it all by myself.

"Okay, then, do it yourself" he replied. I did it myself for sure. I attempted to drive over the huge curb. I went the wrong way, flipping my wheelchair completely over. Laying on the ground, my seat belt still intact, everyone came running. In tears I yelled, " My elbow hurts."

We quickly had to make our way to the Panama City Emergency room. I have been said to be a wimp when it comes to pain. After being checked the doctors said there was nothing broken, except for my ego.

My self-reliant attitude had caused trouble. We live in a society that exalts self-reliance. Risk taking does not always result in something negative, but in this case, it was a lesson well learned.

Often as Christians, we buy into the self-sufficiency myth rather than walking in the freedom of Christ dependency.

I am the vine and you are the branches. Whoever abides in me and I in him, he it is that bears much fruit, for apart from me you can do nothing. John 15:5

If I had allowed my cousin to drive me, or at least guide me in the right direction, then our whole vacation would not have been disrupted by the incident.

When we as believers attempt to accomplish daily tasks in self-sufficiency and pride rather than Christ dependency, we will find one of three scenarios occur. First we may burn out and grow weary. Have you noticed how the hours seem to multiply and you can accomplish more when you commit the task to God. The reverse is true also. If we attempt something in our own efforts we grow exhausted. Our flesh has limitations.

Second, if we attempt to accomplish our destiny apart from God, we will eventually fall, and like with any fall, we are left embarrassed and often hurt.

Third, if we attempt to "do it by ourselves" then we miss the joy of seeing what God is willing to do in and through us that is far greater than our attempts.

The great news is the strength developed through depending upon Christ has no expiration date or statute of limitations.

Philippians 4:13 I can do all things THROUGH CHRIST who strengthens me.

You cannot do this without him, but you can take your *cannot's* to Him.

Heart work:

What have you been trying to do in your own sufficiency? How can you take this to Him and allow Him to strengthen you?

How have you seen God grant you the strength to accomplish something you would have never imagined?

Read 2 Corinthians 12:9. Come alive as you celebrate your can't... thinking about how God's power is made perfect on our weakness.

Day 31 Living Alive

Whew. I cannot believe our 31 day journey has come to an end. I have prayed for you, thought about you, asked God to radically move in your life as I typed each word. I cannot believe this journey is coming to an end. I pray as you walked each day journeying to come alive, that you felt empowered and encouraged to live alive.

I am NOT a gardener. In fact I have been told that mint plants are the kind of plants that you cannot kill—that anyone can grow. Well I have successfully killed mint plants three different times now. I clearly know nothing about keeping a plant alive.

I think the basics are: get some good soil. Plant in the good soil.

Water the plant.

Tend to the plant.

Put the plant in the sun. Unless it does not like that kind of thing. Again. Not a gardener here.

2 Peter 3:18 But GROW in the grace and knowledge of our Lord and Savior Jesus Christ.

Living things are growing things. Living Christians are not stuck in religious rules and routine, but are free as they daily grow in the grace and knowledge of Jesus.

That is my prayer for you. That is my prayer for me. Daily growth in the knowledge of Jesus. I want to plant my heart deep in the good soil—the soil of the Word of God.

As for what was sown on good soil, this is the one who hears the word and understands it. He indeed bears fruit and yields, in one case, a hundredfold. Matthew 13:23

I want to water my heart with living water.

John 4:14 But whoever drinks of the water that I will give him will never be thirsty forever.

Tend to my heart.

Proverbs 4:23 Keep your heart with all vigilance, for from it flow the springs of life.

I pray as you have taken this journey, you have experienced Christ's personal invitation to John 10:10 to come alive and live alive.

Let's not just come alive. Let's live alive.

Romans 6:13 but present yourself to God as those who have been brought from death to LIFE.

Heart work:

How have you come alive? How will you live alive?

ABOUT JENN

Jenn is a coffee loving (well maybe obsessed) Jesus girl. She accepted Christ's invitation to come alive at eight years old and has been so blessed by His love ever since. She is known to go to the playground and swing, go all over the world without a map or a plan, and spoil her nephew and niece rotten.

Jenn has a Master's degree in practical counseling with an emphasis on trauma and spiritual direction. If Jenn could, she would ask you to have a cup of coffee with her at Starbucks and she would ask you what makes you come alive. Jenn is the executive director/keynote speaker for Coming Alive Ministries and is having a blast living her God sized dream. Jenn would love to connect with you at www.comingaliveministries-jenn.com , on Facebook at www.facebook.com/comingaliveministries or on Instagram or twitter as comingalivejenn.

If you are looking for a conference or retreat speaker, Jenn would love to connect with you. E-mail comingaliveministries@gmail.com for more information.

About Coming Alive Ministries

Coming Alive was founded in May 2012 to provide an invitation to Come Alive in Christ through conferences, Christian life coaching, and written resources. We would love to have you join us at one of our Bloom conferences throughout the year. These conferences are designed for ladies age 12-122 to come away for the weekend and connect with Christ through a time of fellowship, worship and the Word.

Connect with us at www.comingaliveministries-jenn.com

CPSIA information can be obtained at www.ICGtesting.com
Printed in the USA
LVOW13s1413130814

398960LV00011B/132/P

9 781496 167644